Turn Over a New Leaf with the Ultimate Cognitive Behavioral Therapy Guide

Essential CBT Techniques and Tools to Change Your
Thoughts and Behavior Patterns Once and for All

LINDA BEXTOR

Disclaimer Notice

The information and techniques described in this book are based on the author's personal experiences and research. The content provided is for general informational purposes only and does not constitute professional advice or replace medical, psychological, or therapeutic treatment.

The author and publisher shall not be held liable for any physical, emotional, psychological, financial, or commercial damages, including but not limited to special, incidental, consequential, or other damages. Readers are advised to consult with a qualified professional or healthcare provider before implementing any suggestions or practices mentioned in this book.

While the utmost care has been taken to ensure the accuracy of the information provided, the author and publisher do not assume responsibility for errors, omissions, or inaccuracies. The author and publisher disclaim any responsibility for any loss or damage arising from the use of the information provided in this book.

It is essential to approach the concepts presented in this book with an open mind and discernment, as each person's journey of healing is unique. The author encourages readers to take responsibility for their well-being and make informed decisions based on their individual circumstances.

First Edition

GET YOUR FREE BONUS

CBT IN ACTION
YOUR DAILY WORKBOOK

To download your Free Bonus scan this **QR Code**

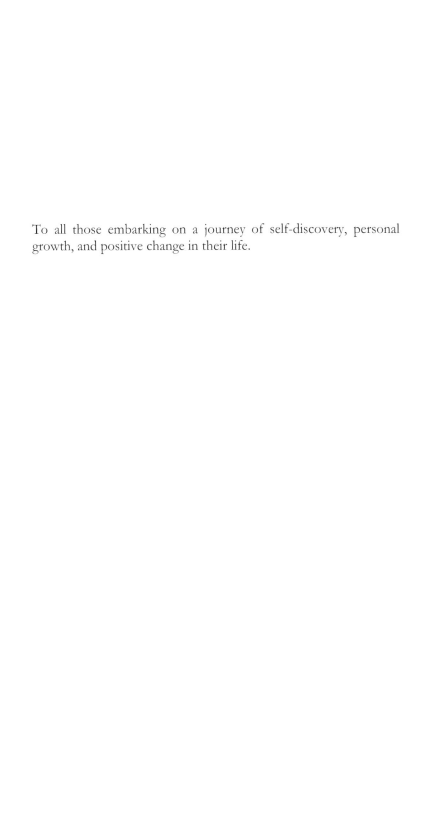

To all those embarking on a journey of self-discovery, personal growth, and positive change in their life.

CONTENTS

INTRODUCTION

Welcome to the fascinating realm of Cognitive Behavioral Therapy (CBT), a powerful, evidence-based approach that empowers you to navigate your thoughts, emotions, and behaviors with newfound control. In this comprehensive guide, we will embark on an enlightening journey of self-discovery, exploring the fundamental principles of CBT, its techniques, and how it can enhance your mental well-being.

Before we embark on this transformative journey, let's establish the purpose and scope of this guide. This book serves as an introduction to CBT and does not claim to be an exhaustive or all-encompassing resource on the subject. While it offers valuable insights and practical tools, it is essential to acknowledge that it cannot replace professional therapeutic treatment. If you are grappling with severe mental health issues or feeling overwhelmed by emotional distress, seeking guidance from a licensed therapist is vital.

The road to change is not always smooth; it requires effort and dedication. Cognitive Behavioral Therapy is no exception. Throughout this voyage, you may encounter obstacles and challenges. Remember that transforming your thoughts and behaviors is a gradual process that demands commitment and time. This guide aims to provide you with a solid foundation and essential tools, but genuine progress might necessitate the support and expertise of a trained therapist.

Now, let us delve into the heart of Cognitive Behavioral Therapy and uncover the empowering principles that underpin its effectiveness.

* * *

Understanding Cognitive Behavioral Therapy (CBT) - The Core Concepts

At its essence, Cognitive Behavioral Therapy is a transformative psychotherapeutic approach that focuses on the intricate interplay between our thoughts, emotions, and behaviors. It operates on the belief that our perceptions of the world, ourselves, and others significantly influence our emotional responses and actions. By gaining a deep understanding of these thought patterns, we can effectively challenge and modify them, leading to profound changes in how we feel and act.

The cognitive component of CBT emphasizes identifying and restructuring negative thought patterns, often termed cognitive distortions. These distortions can result in emotional distress, anxiety, and depression. By learning to recognize and dispute these distortions, individuals can cultivate more rational and balanced thinking, fostering emotional well-being.

The behavioral component of CBT centers on modifying maladaptive behaviors that may perpetuate negative thoughts and emotions. Through a variety of techniques, such as exposure therapy and behavioral experiments, individuals gradually confront their fears and anxieties, empowering themselves to respond more effectively to challenging situations.

* * *

Exploring Cognitive Behavioral Techniques

As we journey through this guide, you will encounter an array of cognitive behavioral techniques thoughtfully designed to equip you with practical tools to navigate life's complexities. Some of these empowering techniques include:

Thought Records: A valuable tool to analyze and reframe negative thoughts. By documenting the negative thought, the associated emotion, and the evidence supporting or challenging the thought, individuals can attain a more balanced perspective.

Graded Exposure: An effective method to confront fears and phobias in a gradual and controlled manner. By repeatedly facing these fears, individuals can diminish their emotional responses and build resilience.

Behavioral Activation: A technique designed to counteract feelings of depression and lethargy by encouraging individuals to engage in rewarding and meaningful activities. By increasing positive experiences, behavioral activation enhances mood and overall well-being.

Problem-solving skills: Teaching individuals effective problem-solving techniques to manage stressful situations and make better decisions.

Relaxation and mindfulness techniques: Helping individuals develop relaxation skills and mindfulness practices to manage stress and promote emotional well-being.

As you embark on the practical application of these techniques in your daily life, remember that change is a gradual process. Be kind to yourself and celebrate even the smallest victories along the way. Embrace the learning process, for it is through these experiences that we grow and evolve.

In addition to the principles and techniques, we have thoughtfully included a complimentary CBT worksheet as a gift to guide you in your journey of self-discovery. This worksheet will prove to be an invaluable tool to implement the teachings of this guide into your life.

In conclusion, this introduction acts as a gateway to the transformative world of Cognitive Behavioral Therapy. Throughout this guide, I aspire to empower you to take charge of your mental well-being and embark on a path of positive change. Embrace the power of CBT and unlock the incredible potential that resides within you.

ABC OF
COGNITIVE BEHAVIORAL THERAPY

What is CBT

Cognitive Behavioral Therapy (CBT) is a widely recognized and evidence-based therapeutic approach that focuses on the relationship between thoughts, emotions, and behaviors. It is a short-term, goal-oriented form of psychotherapy that aims to help individuals understand and change patterns of thinking and behavior that contribute to their psychological difficulties.

CBT operates on the principle that our thoughts, emotions, and behaviors are interconnected, and by identifying and modifying unhelpful patterns, individuals can experience improved mental health and well-being. The therapy is based on the idea that it is not the situations themselves that cause distress, but rather the meanings and interpretations we assign to them.

At the heart of CBT lies the **ABC model**, representing the three critical elements influencing emotional and behavioral responses to events. The Activating Event (A) refers to external situations or triggers that evoke emotions, such as a stressful day at work or a heated argument with a loved one. The Belief System (B) represents our interpretations or beliefs about the activating event. For example, if we believe a professional setback defines us as failures, feelings of worthlessness and sadness may arise. Finally, the Consequence (C) encompasses the emotional and behavioral responses emanating from our belief system. If we perceive ourselves as failures, we may withdraw from social interactions or avoid embracing new challenges.

At its core, CBT operates under the belief that **thoughts significantly influence emotions and behaviors**. By gaining awareness of thought patterns and learning to challenge irrational or unhelpful beliefs, emotional well-being can flourish, leading to positive life changes.

One distinguishing aspect of CBT is its collaborative nature. In a CBT setting, psychologists and individuals work as a team to comprehend and modify thought patterns and behaviors. Psychologists provide guidance, insights, techniques, and support, while individuals actively engage in the process, setting goals, and implementing strategies to achieve positive outcomes.

Central to CBT is the identification and challenging of cognitive distortions—biased and negative thought patterns contributing to emotional distress. Common distortions include all-or-nothing thinking, catastrophizing, and personalization. Recognizing these distortions allows individuals to begin questioning their accuracy and validity.

Following the identification of cognitive distortions, the next step involves thought restructuring. This entails examining evidence for and against the distorted thoughts, leading to the adoption of a more balanced and realistic perspective. This process reduces the emotional intensity of negative thoughts, fostering more positive thinking patterns.

Behavioral activation is another vital aspect of CBT, emphasizing engaging in activities that bring joy and fulfillment. Even during times of low motivation, participating in rewarding activities enhances mood and overall well-being.

Exposure and response prevention represents a highly effective strategy for individuals confronting anxiety disorders. Gradual confrontation of feared situations or stimuli, coupled with preventing anxiety-driven responses, allows individuals to reduce fear and build resilience.

Beyond the therapeutic setting, CBT principles can be applied to daily life, promoting positive change and emotional well-being. By integrating CBT techniques into daily routines, individuals manage stress, cope with challenges, and embrace a more positive outlook on life.

Moreover, CBT recognizes the power of emotional intelligence, enabling individuals to understand and manage their emotions effectively. By developing emotional intelligence, individuals can navigate through challenging situations with grace and resilience, making informed decisions and responding adaptively to life's ups and downs.

In conclusion, Cognitive Behavioral Therapy presents a potent and pragmatic approach to improving mental well-being and fostering personal growth. Through comprehension of the ABC model and embracing CBT's fundamental principles, individuals embark on a transformative journey toward a more fulfilling and optimistic life.

CBT empowers individuals to break free from negative patterns, embracing a more fulfilling and empowered way of living. With dedication and practice, CBT serves as a valuable tool for navigating life's challenges and fostering lasting positive change. Integration of CBT insights and techniques into daily life cultivates emotional resilience, propels personal growth, and reveals the profound impact of this transformative therapy. However, while CBT is effective for many, seeking guidance from licensed psychologists or mental health professionals is essential, particularly for complex or severe psychological issues.

The Origins of Cognitive Behavioral Therapy

Let's now explore the roots of CBT, its development, and how it evolved into a prominent and evidence-based psychotherapeutic method. Whether you are new to CBT or seeking to deepen your understanding, this paragraph will shed light on the history and principles that underpin this empowering therapy.

The groundwork for Cognitive Behavioral Therapy was established by Dr. Aaron T. Beck during the 1960s. As a psychiatrist and psychoanalyst, Dr. Beck noticed the profound impact of his patients' thought patterns on their emotions and behaviors. This pivotal observation marked a crucial turning point in the evolution of CBT, transitioning from a predominantly psychoanalytic perspective to a more cognitive-oriented approach. Dr. Beck's pioneering efforts underscored the importance of cognitive processes in shaping emotional responses, giving rise to the inception of Cognitive Behavioral Therapy.

Initially, CBT focused on treating depression. Dr. Beck introduced the Cognitive Triad, which emphasized three areas of negative thinking commonly observed in depressed individuals: negative perceptions about oneself, the world, and the future. This groundbreaking insight paved the way for cognitive restructuring techniques aimed at challenging and modifying these negative thought patterns. By assisting individuals in recognizing and altering their automatic negative thoughts, CBT demonstrated its effectiveness in reducing depressive symptoms and fostering a more positive mindset.

As CBT evolved, it integrated principles from behavior therapy, which had been gaining momentum in the field of psychology. Behavior therapy emphasized the role of learned behaviors in psychological issues and how modifying these behaviors could lead to positive change. By merging cognitive and behavioral approaches, CBT offered a comprehensive framework to address a wide range of psychological disorders and challenges. This integration became the cornerstone of Cognitive Behavioral Therapy as we know it today.

The "Cognitive Revolution" in psychology during the 1970s marked a significant shift, elevating cognitive approaches to prominence. Psychologists like Albert Ellis and Donald Meichenbaum played instrumental roles in shaping the theoretical underpinnings of CBT through cognitive psychology. Like CBT, Rational emotive behavior therapy (REBT) focused on challenging and replacing irrational beliefs with more rational and constructive thoughts. This cognitive paradigm further solidified CBT's position as a leading therapeutic approach.

Empirical research and clinical trials provided substantial validation for the effectiveness of Cognitive Behavioral Therapy. Researchers conducted studies to assess CBT's efficacy in addressing various psychological mental conditions, such as anxiety disorders, post-traumatic stress disorder (PTSD), and obsessive-compulsive disorder (OCD). Over time, CBT emerged as one of the most extensively researched and evidence-based psychotherapeutic approaches. Its ability to offer short-term, goal-oriented, and enduring change gained widespread recognition in the field of mental health.

As CBT continued to prove its effectiveness, its applications diversified. Therapists adapted CBT techniques to address a wide array of challenges, such as stress management, anger management, and improving self-esteem. CBT also found its way into the realm of personal development and performance enhancement, helping individuals achieve their goals and reach their full potential. This versatility and adaptability further solidified CBT's position as a prominent therapeutic approach.

Today, Cognitive Behavioral Therapy remains a cornerstone of modern psychotherapy, and its principles have been incorporated into various therapeutic modalities. CBT is widely practiced by mental health professionals worldwide, and its applications continue to expand, making it accessible to individuals seeking positive change and personal growth. The enduring impact of CBT on countless lives underscores its significance as a foundational pillar in mental health treatment and personal development.

In conclusion, the origins of Cognitive Behavioral Therapy trace back to the pioneering work of Dr. Aaron T. Beck, who recognized the profound influence of thoughts on emotions and behaviors. The integration of cognitive and behavioral approaches marked a transformative moment in the field of psychotherapy, giving rise to a powerful and evidence-based therapeutic method. As CBT continues to evolve and thrive, its positive impact on countless lives reinforces its status as a foundational pillar in mental health treatment and personal growth.

Traditional CBT vs Positive CBT: Exploring the Contrasts

Traditional CBT and Positive CBT are two variations of this empowering therapeutic approach. Both are rooted in the fundamental principles of CBT, yet they take distinct routes in fostering personal growth and well-being.

* * *

Understanding Traditional CBT

Traditional CBT, the foundational pillar of Cognitive Behavioral Therapy, centers on the identification and challenge of negative thought patterns and behaviors. It operates on the fundamental premise that our thoughts exert a significant influence on our emotions and actions. By acknowledging and modifying cognitive distortions—irrational and negative thoughts—we can foster emotional well-being and positive behavioral changes.

In Traditional CBT, therapists collaboratively explore individuals' thoughts and beliefs, helping them recognize cognitive distortions such as all-or-nothing thinking, overgeneralization, and mind-reading. Through cognitive restructuring, individuals learn to replace negative thoughts with more balanced and constructive ones, leading to improved emotional outcomes and adaptive behaviors.

Proven to be highly effective, Traditional CBT has been successfully applied in treating various psychological conditions, including depression, anxiety disorders, and phobias. It empowers individuals to take control of their thoughts and responses, fostering lasting positive change in their lives.

Introducing Positive CBT

Positive Cognitive Behavioral Therapy (CBT) is an uplifting variation of the traditional CBT approach that accentuates the cultivation of positive emotions and experiences. While both approaches share the fundamental principles of CBT, Positive CBT takes a unique path in promoting well-being and personal growth.

In Positive CBT, individuals learn to recognize and appreciate positive moments in their lives. Through gratitude exercises, mindfulness practices, and positive self-affirmations, individuals can develop a greater sense of well-being and resilience. By focusing on positive experiences, Positive CBT aims to foster a positive outlook and emotional balance.

Moreover, Positive CBT places emphasis on individual strengths and virtues. By identifying and utilizing their unique qualities, individuals gain a newfound sense of self-empowerment. This focus on strengths helps individuals face challenges with confidence and optimism.

The integration of positive elements in the therapeutic process can significantly impact an individual's well-being. Positive CBT complements traditional CBT techniques by offering an avenue for individuals to flourish beyond overcoming difficulties.

It is important to note that Positive CBT is not about dismissing or denying negative emotions. Instead, it encourages individuals to embrace both positive and negative experiences, understanding that experiencing negative emotions is a natural part of life. Positive CBT provides individuals with the tools to navigate these emotions while fostering a balanced perspective.

Overall, Positive CBT presents a valuable opportunity for individuals seeking to enhance their overall well-being, build resilience, and cultivate a positive outlook on life. The integration of positive elements with traditional CBT techniques empowers individuals to not only overcome challenges but also flourish and thrive on their journey of personal growth and positive change.

*** * ***

Blending Positive and Traditional CBT

The integration of Positive CBT with Traditional CBT creates a powerful and comprehensive therapeutic experience. By combining the strengths of both approaches, therapists can offer individuals a well-rounded treatment that addresses negative thought patterns and fosters positive emotions and personal strengths.

Therapists often begin by using Traditional CBT techniques to identify and challenge negative thought patterns and maladaptive behaviors. This process involves exploring cognitive distortions and helping individuals reframe their thoughts to promote emotional well-being. Through substituting negative thoughts with more balanced and constructive ones, individuals can witness substantial enhancements in their emotional responses and behaviors.

As progress is made in addressing negative thought patterns, therapists may introduce elements of Positive CBT to cultivate positive emotions and personal strengths. Encouraging individuals to recognize and savor positive moments in their lives, therapists may incorporate gratitude exercises, mindfulness practices, and positive self-affirmations. By doing so, individuals learn to appreciate positive experiences, leading to a greater sense of well-being and resilience.

The integration of Positive CBT also involves highlighting an individual's unique strengths and virtues. By identifying and utilizing these qualities, individuals can face challenges with confidence and optimism. This focus on strengths empowers individuals to embrace their potential and work towards their goals with a positive mindset.

The blending of Positive and Traditional CBT is not a one-size-fits-all approach. Therapists tailor the therapeutic process to everyone's unique needs and preferences. By doing so, therapists can maximize the positive impact of CBT and create a personalized treatment plan that aligns with an individual's goals.

The collaborative nature of the therapeutic process plays a crucial role in blending Positive and Traditional CBT. Therapists and individuals work together as a team, setting goals and implementing strategies to achieve positive outcomes. This partnership ensures that the therapeutic journey is tailored to an individual's specific needs, leading to more meaningful and lasting change.

Ultimately, the integration of Positive CBT with Traditional CBT provides individuals with a comprehensive and holistic approach to personal growth and well-being. By addressing negative thought patterns while fostering positive emotions and personal strengths, individuals can not only overcome difficulties but also thrive and flourish in their lives.

* * *

Choosing the Right Approach

The choice between Traditional CBT and Positive CBT depends on individual needs and goals. Traditional CBT may be more suitable for individuals struggling with significant negative thought patterns and psychological distress. On the other hand, Positive CBT can be beneficial for those seeking to enhance overall well-being, build resilience, and foster positivity.

Ultimately, the effectiveness of either approach hinges on the collaborative effort between the therapist and the individual. By tailoring the therapeutic process to everyone's unique needs and preferences, therapists can maximize the positive impact of CBT.

To sum up, Cognitive Behavioral Therapy offers two complementary paths: Traditional CBT and Positive CBT. While Traditional CBT focuses on challenging negative thoughts and behaviors, Positive CBT emphasizes cultivating positive emotions and personal strengths. The integration of both approaches, when appropriate, provides a powerful and comprehensive therapeutic experience. Whether overcoming challenges or enhancing overall well-being, CBT offers an empowering journey towards personal growth and positive change.

The 3 Key Principles of Cognitive Behavioral Therapy

The three key principles of CBT are:

1. The Cognitive Principle: Thoughts Influence Emotions and Behaviors

CBT recognizes that our thoughts, beliefs, and interpretations of events significantly impact our emotions and behaviors. The cognitive principle asserts that it is not the situations themselves that cause distress but rather the meanings we assign to them. In other words, it is our thoughts about an event, rather than the event itself, that shape our emotional and behavioral responses. By identifying and challenging negative or irrational thoughts, CBT aims to modify unhelpful thinking patterns and promote healthier emotions and behaviors.

2. The Behavioral Principle: Actions Reinforce and Shape Thoughts and Emotions

CBT acknowledges the influence of behaviors on thoughts and emotions. Our actions can reinforce and maintain certain thought patterns and emotional states. For example, avoiding situations that trigger anxiety can perpetuate the belief that those situations are dangerous. The behavioral principle of CBT emphasizes that engaging in adaptive and constructive behaviors can lead to positive changes in thoughts and emotions. By actively experimenting with new behaviors and engaging in exposure-based techniques, individuals can challenge and modify maladaptive thoughts and emotions.

3. The Collaborative and Goal-Oriented Principle: Active Partnership and Specific Goals

CBT is a collaborative approach that emphasizes a partnership between the therapist and the client. The therapist takes an active role in guiding the therapeutic process, while the client is encouraged to be an active participant in their own recovery. Together, they set specific, measurable, achievable, relevant, and time-bound (SMART) goals that serve as a roadmap for therapy. These goals provide direction and focus for the therapy sessions, enabling both the therapist and client to work towards specific outcomes. The collaborative and goal-oriented principle of CBT empowers individuals to take an active role in their treatment and fosters a sense of ownership and responsibility for their well-being.

These three principles of CBT work in conjunction to guide the therapeutic process. By addressing thoughts, emotions, and behaviors, CBT aims to bring about meaningful change and improvement in individuals' mental health. The principles provide a foundation for the various techniques and strategies employed in CBT, such as cognitive restructuring, behavioral experiments, and problem-solving skills.

* * *

The ABC Model: Understanding the Cognitive Connection

At the heart of Cognitive Behavioral Therapy lies the ABC model, which represents the three essential components that influence our emotional and behavioral responses to events. Let us begin by unraveling the significance of each component.

The A component of the ABC model stands for **Activating Event**, representing external situations or triggers that evoke emotions.

These events can range from everyday occurrences like a job interview or a social interaction to more profound life events, such as the passing of a loved one or a career transition. Each activating event sets the stage for the emotional and behavioral reactions that follow.

The activating event itself does not determine our emotional responses; rather, it is our perception and interpretation of the event that shape our emotional experiences. For example, two individuals faced with the same job interview (the activating event) may have entirely different emotional reactions based on their beliefs and thought processes.

The B component of the ABC model represents our **Belief System**, encompassing our interpretations, thoughts, and cognitive processing related to the activating event. These beliefs can be conscious or unconscious and significantly influence our emotional responses.

Our belief system functions as a filter through which we perceive and understand the world around us. If we hold positive and rational beliefs, we are more likely to experience positive emotions and respond adaptively to challenges. Conversely, negative, and irrational beliefs can lead to emotional distress and maladaptive behaviors.

For instance, consider a job interview as the activating event. If an individual believes that he/she is competent and well-prepared for the interview, he/she may experience confidence and excitement (positive emotions). However, if another individual holds the belief that he/she is not good enough or will inevitably fail, he/she may feel anxious or discouraged (negative emotions).

The C component of the ABC model refers to the **Consequence**, which encompasses the emotional and behavioral responses that arise from our belief system. The consequence is the emotional outcome of our thought patterns and influences how we behave in response to the activating event.

Emotional consequences can span from positive emotions like happiness, joy, and excitement to negative emotions such as fear, sadness, or anger. Behavioral consequences manifest as the actions we take in response to our emotional experiences.

For example, an individual feeling confident after a successful job interview (positive consequence) may express enthusiasm and follow-up with a thank-you email (positive behavior). In contrast, an individual feeling discouraged after a perceived failure in the interview (negative consequence) may withdraw from further job applications (negative behavior).

The ABC model highlights the intricate relationship between our thoughts, emotions, and behaviors. It demonstrates that our perceptions and interpretations of events (activating event) directly influence our emotional responses (belief system) and subsequent actions (consequence).

By becoming aware of this cognitive connection, individuals can gain a deeper understanding of the underlying causes of their emotions and behaviors. Cognitive Behavioral Therapy enables individuals to empower themselves by challenging and modifying cognitive distortions.

By doing so, they can adopt a more balanced and realistic perspective. For example, if an individual believes they will fail in a job interview (B), cognitive restructuring involves examining evidence of their skills and past achievements to challenge the belief

(B) and reduce the emotional intensity of negative thoughts (C).

In conclusion, the ABC model serves as the foundation of Cognitive Behavioral Therapy, offering a profound understanding of the cognitive connection between our thoughts, emotions, and behaviors. By recognizing the influence of our belief system on our emotional responses and actions, individuals can develop emotional resilience and make positive changes in their lives. Cognitive restructuring empowers individuals to challenge cognitive distortions and foster more positive thinking patterns. To embark on a transformative journey towards emotional well-being and personal growth, it is essential that individuals apply the principles of the ABC model in therapy and in their daily lives.

* * *

Cognitive Restructuring: Challenging Negative Thoughts

The process of cognitive restructuring is a vital component of Cognitive Behavioral Therapy (CBT). In this chapter, we will explore the intricacies of cognitive restructuring, understanding its significance, techniques, and the profound impact it can have on fostering emotional well-being and positive behavioral change.

Our thoughts significantly shape our emotional experiences and behaviors. Negative thoughts, when left unexamined, can lead to heightened stress, anxiety, and depression.

The process of cognitive restructuring involves examining the evidence for and against our distorted thoughts, replacing them with more balanced and realistic perspectives. By gaining awareness of our cognitive distortions and challenging them, individuals can foster emotional resilience and a more positive outlook on life.

Cognitive distortions manifest in various forms and frequently represent patterns of thinking that deviate from objective reality. Some common cognitive distortions include all-or-nothing thinking, overgeneralization, mind-reading, catastrophizing, and personalization.

The initial stage of cognitive restructuring involves becoming mindful of our negative thoughts and the situations that trigger them. Maintaining a thought journal can be beneficial in recognizing recurring patterns of negative thinking.

Once negative thoughts are identified, we examine the evidence for and against them. Are there any concrete facts supporting or refuting these thoughts? Often, we realize that our negative thoughts are based on assumptions rather than objective reality.

After examining the evidence, we work to generate more balanced and realistic thoughts. Instead of automatically assuming the worst, we consider alternative, more positive interpretations of the situation.

Like any skill, cognitive restructuring improves with practice. Engaging in the process regularly helps reinforce positive thinking patterns and weaken the influence of negative thoughts.

CBT provides several techniques to facilitate cognitive restructuring. Thought records offer a structured approach to identify, challenge, and modify negative thoughts. Socratic questioning guides individuals in examining the evidence for and against their negative thoughts.

Behavioral experiments involve testing the validity of negative thoughts through behavioral actions. Positive self-affirmations can counteract negative self-talk and strengthen self-confidence and self-esteem.

Cognitive restructuring has a profound impact on an individual's emotional well-being and overall functioning. By challenging negative thoughts and adopting more balanced perspectives, individuals experience decreased emotional distress and enhanced emotional resilience.

Moreover, cognitive restructuring is not limited to the therapeutic setting; it can be applied in daily life to address stressors and promote positive mental health. With practice, individuals become more adept at recognizing and challenging their negative thoughts independently, leading to long-lasting positive change.

* * *

Behavioral Activation: Taking Positive Actions

Behavioral Activation is a fundamental aspect of Cognitive Behavioral Therapy (CBT). In this chapter, we will investigate the significance of Behavioral Activation, its techniques, and how it can lead to positive changes in our lives.

Behavioral Activation is based on the understanding that our behaviors significantly influence our emotions and overall well-being. When individuals are facing challenges such as depression or low motivation, they often withdraw from activities they once enjoyed, leading to a cycle of negative emotions and further withdrawal.

The goal of Behavioral Activation is to break this cycle by encouraging individuals to engage in meaningful and rewarding activities. By taking positive actions and participating in activities that bring joy and fulfillment, individuals can experience improved mood and increased overall satisfaction.

The process of Behavioral Activation begins with identifying activities that align with an individual's values and interests. These activities can be as simple as going for a walk, spending time with loved ones, or pursuing a hobby.

Once identified, individuals are encouraged to schedule these activities into their daily routines. Consistent engagement in positive activities helps individuals build a sense of achievement and mastery over their lives.

Behavioral Activation also involves setting achievable goals. These goals may be small and gradual at first, especially for individuals experiencing depression or low motivation. Celebrating even the smallest accomplishments can boost self-esteem and motivation.

Therapists play a crucial role in supporting individuals through the process of Behavioral Activation. They help individuals identify activities that are personally meaningful and provide encouragement and reinforcement as individuals take steps toward positive change.

Research has shown that Behavioral Activation is an effective treatment for depression and other mood disorders. It offers a practical and accessible approach to improving mood and overall well-being.

Moreover, Behavioral Activation can be easily integrated into daily life, making it a valuable tool for managing stress and enhancing mental health. By taking positive actions and engaging in activities that bring joy, individuals can cultivate a more positive and fulfilling life.

In conclusion, Behavioral Activation is a powerful aspect of Cognitive Behavioral Therapy that encourages individuals to take positive actions and engage in meaningful activities. By breaking the cycle of negative emotions and withdrawal, Behavioral Activation empowers individuals to improve their mood and overall well-being.

Pros and Cons of CBT: An Insight into Cognitive Behavioral Therapy

Cognitive Behavioral Therapy (CBT) is a widely practiced and evidence-based therapeutic approach that has proven effective in treating various psychological conditions. In this chapter, we will explore the pros and cons of CBT, providing you with a balanced understanding of its benefits and limitations.

* * *

Pros of CBT: Harnessing the Power of Cognitive Behavioral Therapy

Cognitive Behavioral Therapy (CBT) has emerged as a highly effective and well-researched therapeutic approach, offering numerous advantages to individuals seeking support for their mental well-being. In this chapter, we will review the key pros of CBT, shedding light on the aspects that make it a valuable and transformative tool in the field of psychotherapy.

1. Evidenced-Based Effectiveness

One of the most notable advantages of CBT is its evidence-based effectiveness. Numerous research studies and clinical trials have consistently demonstrated the positive outcomes of CBT in addressing a wide range of psychological conditions. From depression and anxiety disorders to post-traumatic stress disorder and obsessive-compulsive disorder, CBT has exhibited remarkable results in reducing symptoms and enhancing overall mental health.

2. Goal-Oriented and Time-Limited

CBT is known for its structured and goal-oriented approach. Therapists and individuals collaboratively identify specific goals to work towards during therapy. This time-limited nature of CBT allows individuals to focus on achievable and measurable outcomes. As a result, individuals often experience more immediate positive changes and progress in managing their psychological challenges.

3. Focus on Empowerment

At the core of CBT lies the principle of empowerment. CBT equips individuals with practical tools and techniques to take an active role in managing their thoughts, emotions, and behaviors. Through the therapeutic process, individuals gain a sense of self-efficacy and control over their mental well-being. This empowerment fosters resilience and the ability to navigate future challenges with greater confidence.

4. Adaptable and Tailored Approach

CBT's adaptability is another strength that sets it apart. Therapists can tailor the treatment to suit the unique needs, preferences, and challenges of everyone. While adhering to the foundational principles of CBT, therapists can incorporate other therapeutic modalities when appropriate, making the approach more versatile and comprehensive.

5. Holistic Understanding of Experiences

CBT takes a holistic view of an individual's experiences. It considers the intricate interplay between thoughts, emotions, physical sensations, and behaviors. By addressing this interconnectedness, CBT provides individuals with a comprehensive understanding of their challenges and fosters more effective and sustainable coping strategies.

In conclusion, Cognitive Behavioral Therapy (CBT) offers a range of significant advantages that make it a powerful tool in addressing psychological challenges. Its evidenced-based effectiveness, goal-oriented approach, and focus on empowerment contribute to the positive outcomes observed in many individuals. The adaptability of CBT ensures that it can be tailored to suit individual needs, enhancing its versatility and applicability. Moreover, the holistic understanding of experiences provided by CBT supports individuals in achieving lasting positive changes in their mental well-being.

* * *

Cons of CBT: Acknowledging the Limitations

While Cognitive Behavioral Therapy (CBT) offers numerous advantages, like any therapeutic approach, it also has certain limitations. In this chapter, we will explore the cons of CBT, acknowledging the main aspects that may pose challenges or be less effective for certain individuals.

1. Time and Commitment

CBT requires time and commitment to achieve significant and lasting results. Engaging in therapy and implementing the techniques taught in sessions demands consistent effort and practice. Some individuals may find it difficult to dedicate the necessary time or may struggle to maintain motivation throughout the therapeutic process.

2. Not Suitable for All Conditions

While CBT is highly effective for treating a wide range of psychological conditions, it may not be the best fit for everyone. For certain severe mental health conditions or complex psychological issues, other therapeutic modalities or a combination of approaches may be more appropriate. It is essential for individuals with such conditions to consult with mental health professionals to explore the most suitable treatment options.

3. Emotional Intensity

CBT can involve emotionally intense processes, especially when individuals are required to confront and challenge deeply rooted negative thought patterns or traumas. This emotional intensity may be overwhelming for some individuals, and therapists must be attuned to their clients' needs and emotions during therapy.

4. Focus on Symptoms

Critics of CBT argue that the approach primarily focuses on symptom reduction rather than addressing underlying root causes of psychological distress. While symptom relief is crucial for improving daily functioning, some individuals may benefit from therapeutic approaches that delve deeper into the underlying issues contributing to their challenges.

5. Individual Differences

As with any therapy, CBT may not be equally effective for everyone. Individual differences in personality, coping styles, and personal history can influence how individuals respond to therapy. Therapists must be flexible and adaptive, tailoring the approach to suit the unique needs of each individual.

In conclusion, while Cognitive Behavioral Therapy (CBT) is a highly effective and widely practiced therapeutic approach, it does come with certain limitations. The time and commitment required, the suitability for all conditions, emotional intensity, symptom-focused approach, and individual differences are aspects that both individuals seeking therapy and mental health professionals should consider. By being aware of these cons, therapists can better address potential challenges and tailor the therapy to maximize its effectiveness for everyone.

CBT vs. DBT and ACT: Comparing Three Approaches to Therapy

Having clarified the basic principles of CBT with its pros and cons, let us now delve into the similarities and differences between different therapeutic approaches by shedding light on their strengths and applications. If you are seeking therapy for yourself or someone you care about, understanding these therapies will enable you to make informed decisions on the most suitable approach.

* * *

Cognitive Behavioral Therapy (CBT)

CBT is a widely practiced and evidence-based therapeutic approach that focuses on the connection between thoughts, emotions, and behaviors. The fundamental principle of CBT is that our thoughts influence how we feel and act. By identifying and challenging negative thought patterns, individuals can develop healthier emotional responses and adaptive behaviors.

CBT is goal-oriented and time-limited, making it effective for treating various psychological conditions such as anxiety, depression, and phobias However, over time, it has demonstrated effectiveness in addressing a broader range of emotional dysregulation issues. Therapists work collaboratively with individuals, providing practical tools and techniques to implement in daily life.

* * *

Dialectical Behavior Therapy (DBT)

DBT blends elements of CBT with mindfulness practices and dialectical strategies. It places significant emphasis on validation and acceptance while also encouraging individuals to embrace change and cultivate coping skills.

DBT comprises diverse components, including individual therapy, group skills training, phone coaching, and therapist consultation teams. It empowers individuals with valuable skills to manage distress, regulate emotions, improve interpersonal relationships, and cultivate mindfulness.

* * *

Acceptance and Commitment Therapy (ACT)

ACT focuses on acceptance, mindfulness, and commitment to behavior change. Instead of challenging or altering thoughts, ACT encourages individuals to accept negative thoughts and emotions as part of the human experience.

ACT places emphasis on fostering psychological flexibility, which encompasses being fully present in the moment, making choices aligned with personal values, and relinquishing control over thoughts and emotions.

This approach aims to help individuals align their actions with their values and create a meaningful life. By accepting internal experiences, individuals can reduce the struggle with negative thoughts and emotions, allowing them to pursue a more fulfilling life.

* * *

Similarities and Differences

While CBT, DBT, and ACT share the goal of improving mental well-being, they differ in their theoretical foundations and techniques. CBT primarily targets negative thoughts and behaviors, while DBT places additional emphasis on acceptance and mindfulness. ACT takes acceptance and mindfulness to the forefront, encouraging individuals to live in the present moment.

All three therapies use practical and structured techniques to promote behavioral change and emotional regulation. Additionally, they often involve homework assignments and encourage the active participation of individuals in their therapeutic process.

* * *

Choosing the Right Approach

The choice between CBT, DBT, and ACT depends on individual needs, preferences, and the specific challenges individuals face. While CBT is versatile and widely applicable, DBT may be more suitable for individuals with emotional dysregulation issues, and ACT may resonate with those seeking to develop greater acceptance and mindfulness in their lives.

Collaborating with a qualified mental health professional is of utmost importance when determining the most suitable therapeutic approach. The therapist's expertise and understanding of each individual's unique circumstances play a vital role in tailoring the therapy to maximize its effectiveness.

Each approach has its own unique strengths and applications, and the selection among them depends on individual needs and therapeutic objectives. By gaining insights into these therapies, individuals can make well-informed decisions and embark on a transformative journey towards enhanced mental well-being and personal growth.

THE POWER OF MIND: UNLEASHING THE POTENTIAL OF COGNITIVE BEHAVIORAL THERAPY

Cognitive Behavioral Therapy (CBT) is a therapeutic approach that holds the key to unlocking the immense power of the mind.

The power of the mind is a fascinating and multifaceted concept that encompasses various aspects of human cognition and consciousness. The mind refers to the mental processes and abilities that enable us to think, reason, perceive, imagine, remember, and experience emotions. It plays a crucial role in shaping our thoughts, beliefs, attitudes, behaviors, and overall well-being. Here are some key aspects of the power of the mind:

Perception and Interpretation: Our mind actively processes sensory information from the environment and interprets it based on our past experiences, beliefs, and biases. This subjective interpretation influences our perception of reality and can shape our thoughts and emotions. The power of the mind lies in its ability to influence our subjective experience of the world.

Thoughts and Beliefs: The mind is the birthplace of our thoughts and beliefs. Our thoughts have a profound impact on our emotions, behaviors, and overall mental health. The power of the mind lies in its ability to shape our perception of ourselves, others, and the world around us. By becoming aware of our thoughts and actively challenging negative or unhelpful beliefs, we can harness the power of the mind to promote positive change and well-being.

Mind-Body Connection: The mind and body are intricately interconnected. Our thoughts and emotions can influence our physical sensations and vice versa. Research has shown that positive thoughts and attitudes can have a beneficial impact on physical health, while chronic stress and negative thought patterns can contribute to various physical ailments. By harnessing the power of the mind through practices like meditation, relaxation techniques, and positive self-talk, we can enhance the mind-body connection and promote holistic well-being.

Visualization and Imagery: The mind has the remarkable ability to create and manipulate mental images. Visualization and imagery techniques can be powerful tools for achieving goals, managing stress, and enhancing performance. By vividly imagining positive outcomes and rehearsing desired behaviors in our minds, we can tap into the power of the mind to enhance motivation, confidence, and performance in various domains of life.

Neuroplasticity and Growth: The mind has the capacity to change and adapt throughout our lives. The concept of neuroplasticity refers to the brain's ability to reorganize itself by forming new neural connections. This means that we can actively shape our minds through learning, practice, and intentional mental exercises. By engaging in activities that challenge and stimulate the mind, such as learning new skills, solving puzzles, or engaging in creative endeavors, we can harness the power of neuroplasticity to promote cognitive growth and development.

The power of the mind is an incredible and complex phenomenon that influences our thoughts, emotions, behaviors, and overall well-being. By becoming aware of its potential and actively engaging in practices that harness its power, we can cultivate greater self-awareness, resilience, and personal growth. Whether through cognitive techniques, mindfulness practices, visualization, or other methods, exploring and utilizing the power of the mind can have transformative effects on our lives.

How Your Mind Affects Your Behavior: The Intricate Connection

Cognitive Behavioral Therapy (CBT) holds the key to unleashing the immense power of the mind.

The human mind is a vast landscape of thoughts, emotions, and beliefs, intricately connected to our behaviors and actions. Understanding how our minds influence our behaviors is at the core of Cognitive Behavioral Therapy (CBT), a transformative approach that empowers individuals to take charge of their lives.

Here are some ways in which the mind affects behavior:

Cognitive Processes: Our thoughts and beliefs play a crucial role in shaping our behavior. Our mind processes information, interprets it based on our beliefs and attitudes, and generates thoughts that guide our actions. For example, if we have negative thoughts about our abilities, we may be less likely to take risks or pursue challenging goals. On the other hand, positive and empowering thoughts can lead to more confident and proactive behavior.

Emotional Influence: Emotions, which are a product of our mind, significantly impact our behavior. How we feel in a particular situation can influence our actions and reactions. For instance, if we experience fear, we may avoid certain situations, while feelings of joy or enthusiasm can motivate us to engage in activities. Our emotional state, influenced by our mind, can shape our behavioral responses and choices.

Cognitive Biases: The mind is prone to cognitive biases—systematic errors in thinking that can distort our perception of reality and influence our behavior. Biases such as confirmation bias (favoring information that confirms our existing beliefs) or availability bias (relying on readily available information) can impact decision-making and behavior. Becoming aware of these biases and actively challenging them can help us make more informed and rational choices.

Self-Perception and Identity: Our mind constructs our self-perception and identity, which in turn shape our behavior. How we see ourselves and the beliefs we hold about our abilities, values, and roles influence our actions. For example, if we perceive ourselves as capable and competent, we are more likely to take on challenges and exhibit behavior aligned with those self-perceptions.

Motivation and Goal Setting: Our mind plays a vital role in motivation and goal setting, which directly impact our behavior. Setting specific goals, visualizing desired outcomes, and cultivating a positive mindset can fuel our motivation and drive our behavior toward achieving those goals. Conversely, a lack of motivation or negative thinking patterns can hinder our actions and lead to procrastination or inaction.

Automatic and Unconscious Processes: Our mind operates at both conscious and unconscious levels, influencing behavior in various ways. Automatic and unconscious processes, shaped by our past experiences, can influence our behavior without our conscious awareness. For example, conditioned responses, habits, and implicit biases can guide our actions without us consciously deliberating them.

Self-Regulation: The mind is involved in self-regulation—the ability to manage and control our behavior. It helps us monitor and regulate our actions, impulses, and emotions in alignment with our goals and values. By developing self-awareness and cultivating mindfulness, we can better understand our thoughts and emotions, make intentional choices, and exert self-control over our behavior.

The mind-behavior connection extends beyond the therapeutic setting. In everyday life, our thoughts and beliefs play a crucial role in how we behave. Our self-perception, self-esteem, and self-efficacy directly impact our actions. By nurturing positive self-beliefs and practicing self-compassion, individuals can cultivate a healthier relationship with themselves, leading to more constructive behaviors.

The power of the mind in shaping behavior is evident in habit formation as well. Our thoughts influence our habits, and by changing our thought patterns, we can break free from negative habits and cultivate positive ones.

Cognitive distortions, such as all-or-nothing thinking and catastrophizing, can also influence our behaviors in social interactions. By becoming aware of these distortions and challenging them, individuals can improve their communication skills and build healthier relationships with others.

In the following paragraphs we will consider:

- Most Common Cognitive Distortions
- Top 10 Mental Health Disorders
- Cognitive Skills Improvement Strategies

Most Common Cognitive Distortions

Cognitive distortions, also known as thinking errors or irrational beliefs, are patterns of distorted thinking that can negatively impact our emotions, behaviors, and overall well-being. These distortions often involve automatic and unconscious thoughts that deviate from reality and lead to cognitive biases.

Cognitive distortions are common among individuals, and we may not even be aware of their influence on our lives. By understanding these patterns, we gain the power to challenge and replace them with more rational and balanced thinking. Throughout this article, we will explore various cognitive distortions, such as all-or-nothing thinking, overgeneralization, and personalization, to name a few.

By recognizing these distortions and learning to reframe them, we can cultivate a more positive and constructive mindset, leading to improved emotional well-being and healthier interactions with the world around us.

Here are some of the most common cognitive distortions:

All-or-Nothing Thinking: Also known as black-and-white thinking, this distortion involves viewing situations in extreme, polarized terms. Individuals tend to see things as either perfect or complete failure, with no middle ground. This cognitive distortion can lead to feelings of disappointment, frustration, and self-criticism when things don't turn out exactly as expected.

Overgeneralization: Involves making sweeping and generalized conclusions based on limited evidence or a single negative event. For instance, an individual who experiences failure in a job interview might jump to the conclusion that they are incompetent in all interviews and will never succeed in their career. This cognitive distortion can lead to feelings of hopelessness and impede personal growth.

Mind Reading: Occurs when individuals assume they know what others are thinking or feeling without any concrete evidence. This distortion often leads to misunderstandings, miscommunication, and unnecessary conflict in relationships. People might believe others are judging them negatively, causing social anxiety and isolation.

Discounting the Positive: This cognitive distortion involves dismissing or downplaying positive experiences or qualities, while solely focusing on the negative aspects of oneself or a situation. For instance, when someone receives praise for their work, they may dismiss the compliment, convinced it was insincere or undeserved. By discounting the positive, individuals undermine their self-esteem and fail to recognize their achievements.

Catastrophizing: Entails imagining the worst possible outcomes for a situation, often blowing things out of proportion, and expecting disaster to strike. This cognitive distortion can lead to heightened anxiety and excessive worry, hindering problem-solving and decision-making abilities.

Emotional Reasoning: This involves believing that one's emotions are a reflection of reality. For instance, if someone feels anxious about attending a social event, they might conclude that the event must be dangerous or uncomfortable. Emotional reasoning can lead to avoidance behaviors and limit personal growth.

Should Statements: Should statements involve imposing rigid and unrealistic expectations on oneself or others. These statements often involve words like "should", "must", or "ought to". For example, someone may constantly think, "I should always be perfect" or "Others should always treat me with kindness". This cognitive distortion can lead to feelings of guilt, frustration, and disappointment.

Personalization: Occurs when individuals attribute external events or other people's behaviors to themselves, even when there is no logical connection. For example, if a friend cancels plans, someone might assume it's because they did something wrong. This distortion can lead to self-blame and feelings of inadequacy.

Labeling: Involves applying harsh and negative labels to oneself or others based on a single behavior or mistake. For example, someone who forgets an important appointment might label themselves as "stupid" or "a failure". This distortion can erode self-esteem and contribute to a negative self-image.

Filtering: Also known as mental filtering, this cognitive distortion involves selectively focusing on the negative aspects of a situation while disregarding the positive elements. It's akin to viewing the world through a negative filter, where only the negative aspects are visible. This distortion can lead to a distorted perception of reality and exacerbate feelings of depression and anxiety.

Identifying and challenging these cognitive distortions is the fist step of Cognitive Behavioral Therapy. By acknowledging these patterns, individuals can acquire the ability to challenge their validity and replace them with more balanced and rational thoughts. CBT therapists work collaboratively with their clients to assist them in reframing negative thoughts and fostering healthier cognitive patterns.

It is crucial to bear in mind that cognitive distortions are common and inherent in being human. We all experience moments of irrational thinking. The key lies in recognizing these distortions and taking proactive steps to challenge and modify them. With time and practice, individuals can cultivate a more positive and constructive mindset, leading to enhanced emotional well-being and a heightened sense of resilience.

Understanding the most common cognitive distortions is a fundamental step in the journey of Cognitive Behavioral Therapy. These distortions significantly impact our thoughts, emotions, and behaviors, and recognizing them is crucial for personal growth and improved mental well-being. By challenging these distortions and substituting them with more balanced and realistic thoughts, individuals can experience profound positive changes in their lives. CBT empowers individuals to take control of their minds, leading to a more positive and fulfilling existence.

Top 10 Mental Health Disorders

Cognitive distortions are common elements in various mental health disorders, which are broader and more complex conditions that involve persistent disturbances in mood, cognition, behavior, and often have biological, psychological, and environmental factors at play. While cognitive distortions contribute to the symptoms of mental health disorders, the disorders themselves encompass a wider range of symptoms and challenges that require clinical assessment and intervention. Understanding these disorders is essential, as they can impact individuals from all walks of life.

In this paragraph I will provide a brief description of each disorder, by exploring the symptoms, causes, and available treatment options for each of them. It is important to approach these topics with empathy and sensitivity, as mental health is a crucial aspect of overall well-being. Whether you or someone you know is facing these challenges, gaining knowledge about these disorders can lead to greater understanding and support.

Our main emphasis lies in fostering awareness and eliminating the stigma surrounding mental health. Seeking help for mental health concerns is a courageous step, and professional support can profoundly impact the lives of those affected. Together, let's delve into these top mental health disorders, empowering ourselves with knowledge and compassion to promote mental wellness within our communities.

1. Depression: Depression is a mood disorder marked by enduring sadness, loss of interest or pleasure, and feelings of hopelessness. It affects millions of people worldwide and can impact daily functioning, relationships, and overall quality of life. Biological factors, life events, and genetics can contribute to its development.

Treatment options include psychotherapy, medication, and lifestyle changes.

2. Anxiety Disorders: Anxiety disorders encompass a range of conditions like generalized anxiety disorder (GAD), panic disorder, social anxiety disorder, and specific phobias. Individuals with anxiety disorders experience excessive worry, fear, or nervousness, often leading to avoidance behaviors. Cognitive-behavioral therapy (CBT), exposure therapy, and medication are common treatments.

3. Bipolar Disorder: Bipolar disorder involves extreme mood swings, including depressive episodes and manic episodes. During manic episodes, individuals may experience heightened energy, impulsivity, and grandiosity. Medication and psychotherapy, such as CBT and family-focused therapy, are essential for managing symptoms.

4. Schizophrenia: Schizophrenia is a chronic and severe mental disorder that affects how a person thinks, feels, and behaves. Hallucinations, delusions, and disorganized thinking are common symptoms. Treatment often involves a combination of antipsychotic medication, psychosocial therapies, and support services.

5. Post-Traumatic Stress Disorder (PTSD): PTSD (Post-Traumatic Stress Disorder) can develop after exposure to or witnessing a traumatic event. Common symptoms include flashbacks, nightmares, and hypervigilance. Therapeutic methods like Cognitive Processing Therapy (CPT) and Eye Movement Desensitization and Reprocessing (EMDR) help individuals process distressing memories related to the trauma.

6. Obsessive-Compulsive Disorder (OCD): Obsessive-Compulsive Disorder (OCD) is distinguished by intrusive and distressing thoughts (obsessions) along with repetitive behaviors or mental acts (compulsions). The gold standard treatment for OCD is cognitive-behavioral therapy, particularly exposure and response prevention (ERP), which proves highly effective in managing the condition.

7. Eating Disorders: Eating disorders, such as anorexia nervosa, bulimia nervosa, and binge-eating disorder, involve unhealthy relationships with food and body image. Treatment often includes psychotherapy, nutrition counseling, and medical monitoring.

8. Attention-Deficit/Hyperactivity Disorder (ADHD): ADHD is a neurodevelopmental disorder identified by symptoms of inattention, hyperactivity, and impulsivity. Common approaches to managing ADHD symptoms include behavioral therapy, medication, and providing support at school and home.

9. Borderline Personality Disorder (BPD): BPD (Borderline Personality Disorder) is characterized by unstable moods, self-image, and relationships. Individuals with BPD may face challenges with intense emotions and impulsive behaviors. Dialectical Behavior Therapy (DBT) is a specialized and effective treatment approach for BPD.

10. Substance Use Disorders: Substance use disorders refer to the misuse of alcohol, drugs, or other substances, resulting in substantial impairment in daily life. Treatment may include detoxification, counseling, support groups, and medication-assisted therapy.

It is crucial to approach these mental health disorders with empathy and understanding. Treatment options may include psychotherapy, medication, or a combination of both. Early intervention and support from mental health professionals can greatly improve outcomes.

Always bear in mind that mental health is just as crucial as physical health, and seeking help for mental health concerns is a courageous demonstration of strength. If you or someone you know is experiencing mental health challenges, don't hesitate to seek guidance and support from a qualified professional. Together, we can strive towards promoting mental well-being and dismantling the stigma surrounding mental health.

Cognitive Skills Improvement Strategies

Regardless of the mental conditions, be it simple behavioral distortions or more serious mental health problems, it is crucial that individuals constantly work on improving their cognitive abilities as part of a therapeutic process.

We will now explore practical strategies and techniques rooted in CBT principles to boost your cognitive abilities and optimize your mental performance. Whether you want to enhance your memory, sharpen your focus, or improve your problem-solving skills, these evidence-based approaches can be invaluable tools in your cognitive toolkit.

- **Mindfulness Meditation**

Mindfulness meditation is a powerful technique to improve cognitive skills by cultivating awareness of the present moment. Regular practice can enhance attention, focus, and working memory. Studies have shown that mindfulness practices can lead to structural changes in the brain associated with improved cognitive function.

- **Cognitive Training Games**

Participating in cognitive training games and exercises can stimulate your brain and facilitate neuroplasticity, which is the brain's capacity to reorganize and establish new neural connections. Games that target memory, attention, and problem-solving can be beneficial for enhancing cognitive skills.

- **Mental Stimulation**

Keeping your mind active through continuous learning and intellectual challenges can bolster cognitive abilities. Reading, learning a new language, or engaging in hobbies that require critical thinking can stimulate brain function and cognitive growth.

- **Regular Exercise**

Physical exercise not only benefits your body but also positively impacts your brain. Aerobic exercises have been linked to improved cognitive function, memory, and attention. Physical exercise boosts blood flow to the brain and stimulates the release of neurotransmitters that contribute to cognitive health.

- **Sleep and Rest**

Quality sleep is essential for optimal cognitive function. During sleep, the brain consolidates memories and processes information. Ensure you get enough restful sleep to enhance cognitive performance during waking hours.

- **Balanced Diet**

A well-balanced diet, rich in nutrients, antioxidants, and omega-3 fatty acids, plays a vital role in preserving brain health. Specific foods, like blueberries, walnuts, and fatty fish, have been linked to enhanced cognitive function.

- **Stress Management**

Long-term stress can negatively affect cognitive function. Integrating stress-reduction techniques, like deep breathing, progressive muscle relaxation, and CBT-based stress management, can enhance cognitive well-being.

- **Setting Realistic Goals**

Breaking tasks into smaller, manageable goals can improve focus and motivation. Celebrate your achievements along the way to boost self-confidence and maintain a positive mindset.

- **Social Engagement**

Meaningful social interactions and relationships are beneficial for cognitive health. Engaging in conversations, social activities, and group settings can stimulate cognitive function and emotional well-being.

- **Seeking Professional Support**

If you encounter significant cognitive challenges or cognitive decline, seeking professional evaluation and support is essential. A qualified mental health professional can assess your cognitive abilities and provide targeted interventions or therapies as needed.

Remember that improving cognitive skills is a gradual process that requires consistency and patience. Incorporate these strategies into your daily routine and adjust them to fit your individual needs and preferences. As you practice and refine these techniques, you may notice enhanced cognitive abilities, improved mental clarity, and an overall positive impact on your daily life.

Reclaiming Your Inner Child through CBT

Before moving on to the description of exercises to put into practice what has been learned so far, it is useful to make a final mention of how CBT can also be useful in the healing process of the inner child.

* * *

Understanding the Inner Child

The concept of the inner child is an essential aspect of self-awareness and personal growth in Cognitive Behavioral Therapy (CBT). It refers to the emotional experiences and beliefs that we developed during our formative years, typically in childhood. These early experiences play a profound role in shaping our beliefs, self-perception, and emotional responses as adults.

The inner child encompasses both positive and negative experiences. Positive experiences, such as love, nurturing, and validation, contribute to emotional resilience and a positive self-image. However, negative experiences, like trauma, neglect, or emotional abuse, can lead to emotional wounds that may impact our adult lives. These wounds might manifest as self-doubt, low self-esteem, fear of rejection, or difficulty forming healthy relationships.

* * *

The Inner Child and CBT

CBT recognizes the significance of the inner child in influencing our thoughts, emotions, and behaviors. By understanding and addressing the emotional wounds from our past, we can begin the healing process. CBT techniques, such as imagery rescripting, allow us to revisit past experiences and provide emotional support to our inner child, fostering healing and growth.

Embracing the concept of the inner child requires self-compassion and vulnerability. It involves acknowledging the impact of past experiences without judgment or blame. Through CBT, we learn to treat ourselves with kindness and understanding, creating a safe space to explore and heal our inner child's emotional wounds.

As we reconnect with our inner child, we develop a deeper understanding of ourselves and our emotional needs. This newfound self-awareness empowers us to build healthier relationships and create a more fulfilling life. By nurturing and reclaiming our inner child, we can break free from self-limiting beliefs and embrace the joy and authenticity of our true selves.

* * *

Healing the Inner Child

Within the domain of Cognitive Behavioral Therapy (CBT), healing the inner child assumes a significant role in promoting emotional well-being and personal growth. The inner child embodies the emotional experiences and beliefs developed during childhood, which can persistently influence thoughts and behaviors in adulthood. CBT recognizes the significance of addressing unresolved childhood issues and traumas to alleviate cognitive distortions and maladaptive coping strategies. By nurturing and healing the inner child through cognitive restructuring and behavioral interventions, individuals can gain a deeper understanding of their emotional triggers and develop healthier ways of responding to life's challenges. This healing process empowers individuals to cultivate emotional resilience and embrace a more positive and fulfilling life journey.

If you would like to learn more about inner child healing, you will find a lot of useful information in my other book "How To Heal Your Inner Child: Take Back Control of Your Life Immediately and Reach Your Full Potential by Setting Yourself Free from Negative Patterns and Connecting with Authentic Emotions", which offers insights and practical advice to set free from unhealthy behavioral patterns and recover from your past wounds, as well as lots of strategies to effectively manage intense emotional reactions in your daily life.

Benefits of Reclaiming Your Inner Child

The benefits of reclaiming your inner child through CBT are numerous:

Emotional Freedom: Healing the inner child liberates us from past emotional burdens, allowing us to experience emotional freedom and resilience.

Authenticity: Reconnecting with our inner child enables us to live more authentic and fulfilling lives, aligning our actions with our true desires and values.

Improved Relationships: As we heal our inner child, we develop healthier relationships with ourselves and others, fostering greater intimacy and connection.

Empowerment: Reclaiming our inner child empowers us to break free from self-limiting beliefs and embrace our potential.

Emotional Regulation: Understanding and processing emotions from our inner child's perspective equips us with effective emotional regulation skills.

Reclaiming your inner child through CBT is a journey of self-discovery, healing, and personal growth. By integrating CBT techniques into your life, you can transform negative thought patterns, heal emotional wounds, and embrace the joy and authenticity of your inner child. Nevertheless, seeking professional guidance from a qualified CBT therapist can provide invaluable support on your path to reclaiming your inner child and living a more fulfilling and meaningful life.

ESSENTIAL CBT
TECHNIQUES AND TOOLS

Introduction

Now that it is clear what CBT is and how it can help you, in this section I want to equip you with practical techniques and invaluable tools to enhance your mental well-being.

In a world that often feels like a whirlwind of thoughts and emotions, CBT stands as a guiding light, offering a structured approach to understanding and managing the complexities of the human mind. This guide is designed to provide insights and tools that can pave the way to positive change, it's crucial to underscore that it doesn't substitute professional therapeutic intervention. For those grappling with severe mental health challenges, seeking guidance from licensed therapists remains a crucial step toward comprehensive healing.

At its core, CBT embraces the idea that our thoughts, emotions, and behaviors are interconnected threads that weave the fabric of our psychological experiences. It acknowledges the impact of thoughts on emotions and behaviors, and vice versa. Through this lens, CBT facilitates a profound understanding of how **altering our thought patterns can lead to tangible changes in our emotions and actions**.

One fundamental aspect of CBT is the **identification of automatic thoughts**—those swift, sometimes unnoticed, cognitions that influence our reactions. These automatic thoughts have the power to shape our emotional responses and steer our behavior. CBT introduces the concept of thought journaling, a tool that empowers you to record these fleeting thoughts when distressing emotions arise. This practice unveils the hidden currents of your mind, enabling you to recognize patterns and uncover the underlying triggers of your emotions.

CBT goes beyond mere identification; it's about **challenging and reshaping these automatic thoughts**. The tool of Socratic questioning becomes your ally, guiding you to critically examine the validity of your thoughts. Through a series of thought-provoking questions, you can dismantle negative thought patterns, fostering a more balanced and realistic perspective on challenging situations.

Yet, CBT extends beyond the confines of the mind—it acknowledges the role of behaviors in shaping our mental experiences. Behavioral experiments, a cornerstone of CBT, encourage you to step outside your comfort zone and test the validity of your beliefs. By gradually exposing yourself to feared situations, you gather firsthand evidence that contradicts your negative assumptions, ultimately diminishing their hold on you.

In your journey toward lasting transformation, CBT equips you with coping strategies to weather life's storms. Coping cards, adorned with affirmations, soothing phrases, and healthy coping mechanisms, serve as tangible reminders of your resilience during moments of challenge and uncertainty.

As you delve into this guide, remember that CBT is a process—a path that requires dedication and effort. While the tools and techniques outlined here provide a sturdy foundation, enlisting the support of a qualified therapist can amplify your progress.

In the chapters that follow, we'll explore each technique and tool in depth, offering insights, practical steps, and real-world examples. Armed with knowledge and the power to reshape your cognitive landscape, you're embarking on a journey that holds the promise of enhanced mental well-being and a renewed sense of self.

What we will see:

o Practical Exercises for Self-Practice

o Helpful Tips for Identifying and Challenging Negative Thoughts

o CBT and Mindfulness: A Synergy for Self-Discovery and Resilience

o 7 Effective Strategies to Change Thinking Patterns

o CBT for Anger Management

o 3 CBT Techniques to Manage Anxiety and Work Stress

o CBT for Eating Disorders: Navigating a Path to Recovery

o How to Apply CBT Techniques to Any Other Mental Health and Stress-Related Disorder

o Relapse Prevention: Sustaining Progress Beyond Therapy

Practical Exercises for Self-Practice

The following exercises are designed to empower you on your path to enhanced mental well-being. These exercises offer a hands-on approach to applying CBT principles in your daily life, allowing you to actively engage with your thoughts, emotions, and behaviors. While not a substitute for professional therapy, these exercises can serve as invaluable tools for personal growth and self-improvement.

Each exercise within this collection is grounded in CBT's core philosophy—recognizing the interplay between thoughts, emotions, and behaviors. By participating in these exercises, you'll gain insights into your thought patterns, challenge negative beliefs, confront fears, and foster self-compassion. The goal is to enable you to take an active role in shaping your cognitive landscape and developing skills that contribute to your emotional resilience.

From thought journaling to exposure practice, from cognitive restructuring to self-compassion cultivation, these exercises provide you with the opportunity to actively engage with your inner world. As you embark on this journey of self-exploration and empowerment, keep in mind that these exercises are tools you can integrate into your daily routine. They offer a window into the transformative potential of CBT, empowering you to navigate life's challenges with greater insight and emotional balance.

Remember that while these exercises offer a valuable framework for self-improvement, they are most effective when approached with an open mind, a willingness to learn, and a commitment to self-care. As you delve into each exercise, consider how it aligns with your personal goals and aspirations. By embracing these practices, you are taking a proactive step towards enhancing your mental well-being and fostering a deeper understanding of yourself.

* * *

Thought Journaling: Unveiling the Mind's Inner Workings

Thoughts often arise spontaneously, guiding our emotional responses and actions. Engaging in thought journaling, a cornerstone exercise of CBT, empowers you to bring these thoughts to light. When distressing emotions surface, take a moment to jot down the situation that triggered the emotion, the emotions you experienced, and the thoughts that accompanied them. As you consistently engage in thought journaling, patterns will emerge. By recognizing recurring thought patterns, you can begin to challenge and reframe them, ultimately leading to more adaptive emotional responses.

* * *

Cognitive Restructuring: Shifting Perspectives

Negative thoughts can create a lens through which we perceive the world, influencing our emotional experiences. Cognitive restructuring is an exercise designed to help you challenge and reshape these negative thought patterns. When you catch yourself experiencing a negative thought, take a step back and evaluate it critically. Ask yourself whether there is concrete evidence supporting the thought or if it is based on assumptions. For example, you might ask, "Is this thought based on facts or assumptions?" or "What evidence do I have that supports or contradicts this thought?". By introducing a more balanced perspective and considering alternative interpretations, you can reduce the emotional impact of negative thoughts.

* * *

Exposure Practice: Confronting Fears Gradually

Facing our fears is an integral part of personal growth and emotional resilience. While this guide doesn't replace professional exposure therapy, it introduces a simplified version of exposure practice that you can incorporate into your self-care routine. Begin by identifying a fear or situation you've been avoiding due to anxiety. Create a hierarchy of exposure, starting from situations that induce mild discomfort and gradually progressing to more anxiety-provoking scenarios. By systematically exposing yourself to these situations, you can desensitize your emotional response over time, leading to increased confidence and reduced anxiety.

* * *

Decatastrophizing

This technique helps you challenge catastrophic thinking by asking questions like "What's the evidence that this worst-case scenario will actually happen?" and "What's the worst thing that could realistically happen, and how would I cope with it?". By exploring alternative possibilities, you gain a clearer view of the situation, often realizing that the extreme outcome is unlikely. Essentially, decatastrophizing assists you in reining in exaggerated fears and tackling challenges with a more realistic mindset. It's a tool to prevent unnecessary worry and reduce the emotional impact of potential worst-case scenarios.

* * *

Behavioral Activation Planning

Behavioral activation involves scheduling and engaging in activities that you enjoy and that give you a sense of accomplishment. By listing enjoyable and fulfilling activities, you create a schedule that ensures you engage in these activities regularly. This practice counteracts the tendency to withdraw from things you once enjoyed due to depression. By setting achievable goals and gradually reintroducing pleasurable activities into your routine, you boost your mood, increase your sense of accomplishment, and create positive experiences. This technique is like a step-by-step guide to breaking free from the cycle of inactivity and low mood that often accompanies depression.

* * *

Gratitude Journaling

Gratitude journaling is a practice where you regularly jot down three things you are thankful for. These can range from simple pleasures to significant events. It's about focusing on the positive aspects of your life and acknowledging them. For each item, briefly note why you appreciate it. This exercise helps shift your mindset towards positivity, reducing stress and increasing overall well-being. By consistently acknowledging the good things, you develop a habit of noticing and savoring positivity in everyday life. This practice is shown to improve mood, relationships, and even sleep quality. Simply put, it's a way to cultivate gratitude and bring more positivity into your daily routine.

* * *

Self-Compassion Cultivation: Nurturing Your Inner Self

CBT places significant emphasis on self-compassion—an essential practice that encourages treating oneself with the same kindness and understanding as one would offer to a close friend. Engage in self-compassion exercises to cultivate a more nurturing and supportive relationship with yourself. Consider writing yourself a compassionate letter, acknowledging your strengths and challenges without self-judgment. By practicing self-compassion, you can counteract self-criticism, enhance self-esteem, and foster emotional resilience.

As you embark on this journey of self-exploration through CBT exercises, remember the context in which these exercises are offered. While they can be valuable tools for personal growth and self-improvement, they are not a replacement for comprehensive therapeutic support when needed. Professional therapists possess the expertise to tailor interventions to your unique needs, especially for complex issues.

Approach these exercises with curiosity, openness, and a willingness to learn about yourself. Embrace the insights they offer and integrate them into your daily routine. By engaging with these exercises, you embark on a path of self-awareness, personal growth, and enhanced emotional well-being.

Helpful Tips for Identifying and Challenging Negative Thoughts

In the vast expanse of our minds, thoughts continuously ebb and flow, shaping our emotional experiences and behaviors. However, amidst the cacophony of thoughts, some carry the weight of negativity, influencing our perception of self, others, and the world around us. The realm of Cognitive Behavioral Therapy (CBT) offers a profound exploration into these negative thought patterns, unraveling their impact and presenting strategies to reshape their influence.

At the core of CBT lies the recognition that our thoughts are not absolute truths, but rather interpretations colored by our unique perspectives. These interpretations can sometimes veer into distorted territory, magnifying problems, emphasizing the worst outcomes, and diminishing our abilities. CBT introduces the concept of cognitive distortions, those subtle yet powerful shifts that taint our thinking.

To navigate this intricate terrain, CBT introduces the thought record technique (Thought Journaling). Imagine it as a magnifying glass that brings these automatic thoughts into focus. By dissecting the triggering event, the ensuing thought, associated emotions, and supporting evidence, we begin to unravel the threads of negative thinking. This analytical process exposes the gaps between perception and reality, illuminating the areas where our thoughts may have strayed from the truth.

Guiding us further along this journey, Socratic questioning comes into play. Channeling the spirit of the ancient philosopher, we engage in a dialogue with ourselves, gently probing the validity of our negative thoughts. Are they grounded in evidence? Could alternative explanations exist? This process challenges the initial judgments, ushering in a broader perspective that often unveils the fallacies in our initial assumptions.

As we unravel the layers of negative thinking, it becomes evident that these patterns are not indomitable truths but malleable constructs. CBT equips us with the tools to transform these patterns, enabling us to intercept, challenge, and reframe negative thoughts before they spiral into overpowering emotions and counterproductive actions.

By embracing the techniques offered by CBT, we embark on a journey of empowerment and self-discovery. With each thought identified and dissected, we move closer to understanding the intricate relationship between thoughts, emotions, and behaviors. The power to reshape our cognitive landscape lies within our grasp, a power that CBT can unlock, facilitating a more balanced and optimistic outlook on life.

CBT and Mindfulness: A Synergy for Self-Discovery and Resilience

In the intricate realm of the human mind, two powerful practices—Cognitive Behavioral Therapy (CBT) and mindfulness—converge to offer a transformative journey of self-improvement. This chapter, titled "CBT and Mindfulness", delves into the harmony between these approaches and how their integration can pave the way for emotional resilience, self-awareness, and balanced well-being.

Imagine CBT and mindfulness as two intertwined streams, each contributing distinct perspectives to the landscape of our thoughts and emotions. CBT's focus on restructuring negative thought patterns aligns with mindfulness' call for nonjudgmental observation of these thoughts. Together, they forge a comprehensive framework that encourages us to engage with our internal experiences compassionately.

This integration holds profound benefits. The structured techniques of CBT empower us to recognize and challenge detrimental thought patterns, providing a solid foundation for managing conditions like anxiety and depression. Mindfulness, complementing these efforts, encourages a state of present-moment awareness that enables us to observe our thoughts without attachment.

Relaxation techniques serve as bridges between CBT and mindfulness, offering solace in a fast-paced world. Deep breathing techniques ground us in the rhythm of our breath, progressively calming our minds. Concurrently, progressive muscle relaxation fosters harmony between our bodies and minds, reducing physical tension. Guided imagery transcends both practices, guiding us to imaginary havens that offer respite from daily stresses.

At the heart of this synergy lies mindfulness meditation—a practice embodying the essence of both CBT and mindfulness. During mindfulness meditation, we gently observe our thoughts, letting them drift without judgment, cultivating emotional regulation and heightened self-awareness.

In essence, the partnership between CBT and mindfulness illuminates a journey of personal growth and emotional healing. This integration equips us with tools to navigate our thoughts and emotions while anchoring us in the present moment with empathy.

* * *

Exploring Relaxation Techniques: A Journey to Inner Calm

Amid the hustle and bustle of modern life, a sanctuary of tranquility awaits through various relaxation techniques. Let me introduce you to a diverse array of relaxation practices—deep breathing, progressive muscle relaxation, guided imagery, and mindfulness meditation. These techniques, each a unique pathway to inner calm, offer respite from the demands of daily life and contribute to your holistic well-being.

1.   Deep Breathing: Navigating the Rhythm of Breath

Imagine a simple yet profound practice that can instantly shift your state of mind. Deep breathing invites you to reconnect with the innate rhythm of your breath, anchoring you in the present moment. With each inhale and exhale, stress dissipates, and a sense of calm washes over you. This technique is accessible anywhere, serving as a portable oasis of relaxation in the midst of life's challenges.

2.   Progressive Muscle Relaxation: Unraveling Tension

Our bodies often mirror the stress we carry within. Progressive muscle relaxation guides you through a systematic process of tensing and releasing muscle groups, shedding physical tension like a well-worn coat. This technique fosters a profound mind-body connection, teaching you to distinguish between tension and relaxation and equipping you with the ability to release stress at will.

3.   Guided Imagery: Escaping to Serenity

Guided imagery transports you to serene landscapes of your creation, offering a mental escape from the demands of reality. As you close your eyes, you're guided through scenes rich with sensory details—a peaceful beach, a lush forest, or a tranquil meadow. Through the power of imagination, you can release stress, cultivate positive emotions, and harness the healing potential of your mind's eye.

4.   Mindfulness Meditation: Embracing the Present Moment

At the heart of this exploration lies mindfulness meditation—a practice that melds seamlessly with the principles of CBT. Mindfulness meditation encourages you to sit in stillness, observing your thoughts without judgment. This practice fosters emotional regulation, self-awareness, and an appreciation for the richness of the present moment. With regular practice, mindfulness meditation becomes a wellspring of calm that you can tap into whenever needed.

* * *

Embracing the Wholeness

As you venture further into the realm of relaxation techniques, a profound realization dawns—an understanding that these practices are not mere isolated tools but interconnected threads that weave a tapestry of well-being. Just as CBT and mindfulness harmonize, the techniques of deep breathing, progressive muscle relaxation, guided imagery, and mindfulness meditation work in concert to create a holistic approach to emotional balance and self-care.

Imagine yourself embarking on a journey, where each technique is a steppingstone that contributes to your overall resilience and mental clarity. The rhythmic dance of deep breathing calms your mind, inviting you to be present in every inhale and exhale. Progressive muscle relaxation releases not just the physical tension held within your body but also the mental burdens that accompany it. Guided imagery allows your imagination to roam free, constructing landscapes of serenity and grace that become a refuge from stress. Mindfulness meditation, with its invitation to embrace the present moment, is the compass that guides you back to your center whenever life's chaos threatens to pull you off course.

This harmonious integration invites you to move beyond the notion of relaxation techniques as standalone exercises. Instead, they become threads woven into the fabric of your daily routine—threads that, when pulled together, create a tapestry of inner calm, emotional regulation, and self-awareness.

As you practice each technique, consider them as chapters in a larger story—the story of your journey toward well-being. Just as a symphony is composed of individual notes that blend to create harmony, your journey is composed of these techniques that blend to create a harmonious life. Each technique offers its unique melody—a melody that resonates with your essence and guides you toward a deeper understanding of yourself.

As you continue to explore the intricate interplay of CBT, mindfulness, and relaxation techniques, remember that this is a journey of self-discovery and empowerment. This integration empowers you to navigate the ebb and flow of life with grace, resilience, and an unwavering sense of inner peace. By embracing the wholeness of these practices, you forge a path toward a balanced and enriched life—one where your thoughts, emotions, and actions align harmoniously, and where you become the conductor of your own symphony of well-being.

7 Effective Strategies to Change Thinking Patterns

In the intricate tapestry of our minds, thoughts weave the threads that shape our perceptions, emotions, and behaviors.

Cognitive Behavioral Therapy (CBT) offers a transformative journey toward understanding and reshaping these thinking patterns. These strategies aim to guide you through practical techniques that empower you to navigate the labyrinth of your thoughts and cultivate a more positive and resilient mindset.

1. Recognize Automatic Negative Thoughts

Imagine a world where your thoughts take center stage—an inner dialogue that often goes unnoticed. The first step in changing thinking patterns is to become an observer of your thoughts. Notice when negative thoughts arise, like self-doubt or pessimism. By recognizing these automatic patterns, you gain power over them.

Automatic negative thoughts can be subtle. They might creep into your mind during moments of uncertainty or self-criticism. For instance, you might find yourself thinking, "I'll never succeed in this task" or "I always mess things up". These thoughts can shape your beliefs and influence your behavior, leading to a self-fulfilling prophecy.

2. Challenge and Reframe

Just as a sculptor molds clay, you can reshape your thoughts.

Challenge the validity of negative thoughts by asking, "Is this thought based on evidence?". Challenge irrational beliefs with logic and evidence, fostering a shift toward more balanced thinking. Reframe negative self-talk into realistic and compassionate statements.

For example, let's say you receive feedback on a project at work that isn't entirely positive. Instead of immediately thinking, "I'm terrible at my job", challenge this thought. Ask yourself if there's evidence to support this belief. Perhaps you've received positive feedback in the past or have successfully completed similar projects. Reframe the negative self-talk into a more balanced perspective like, "I may have areas to improve, but I also have strengths that I can build on".

3. Practice Mindfulness

Mindfulness invites you to embrace the present moment without judgment. By practicing mindfulness, you cultivate awareness of your thoughts without attachment. This technique encourages you to observe your thoughts as passing clouds in the sky, reducing their impact on your emotions.

Mindfulness can be incorporated into your daily routine. Take a few moments each day to sit quietly and focus on your breath. When thoughts arise, acknowledge them without judgment and gently bring your attention back to your breath. Over time, this practice enhances your ability to observe your thoughts without being overwhelmed by them.

4. Cultivate Self-Compassion

Imagine treating yourself as you would a close friend—with kindness and understanding. Self-compassion involves acknowledging your flaws without harsh self-criticism. This practice counteracts the negative self-talk that can perpetuate negative thinking patterns.

To cultivate self-compassion, start by acknowledging your own humanity. Remember that making mistakes is part of being human, and everyone faces challenges. Treat yourself with the same kindness and understanding you would offer to a friend who is struggling. Instead of berating yourself for a mistake, offer words of comfort and encouragement.

5. Focus on Solutions

Imagine shifting your perspective from problems to solutions. When faced with challenges, redirect your energy toward brainstorming and implementing solutions. This approach empowers you to take control of your circumstances, breaking the cycle of rumination.

Instead of dwelling on a problem, actively engage your problem-solving skills. Identify potential solutions and consider their pros and cons. Taking action to address challenges not only shifts your mindset but also leads to a sense of accomplishment and empowerment.

6. Challenge Catastrophic Thinking

Catastrophic thinking magnifies the worst possible outcome of a situation. Challenge this pattern by evaluating the realistic likelihood of such outcomes. Imagine adopting a more balanced perspective that considers a range of possible outcomes, reducing anxiety and fostering resilience. For instance, if you're anxious about an upcoming presentation, challenge the catastrophic thought that you'll completely forget your lines and embarrass yourself. Consider the times you've successfully given presentations in the past or the preparation you've done for this one. This more balanced perspective can alleviate anxiety and help you approach the situation with greater confidence.

7. Embrace Gratitude and Positivity

Imagine reframing your focus toward what's going well in your life. Practicing gratitude invites you to identify and appreciate positive aspects. By shifting your attention from what's lacking to what's present, you foster a mindset of positivity. Each day, take a moment to reflect on the things you're grateful for. They can be simple pleasures like a warm cup of tea or a supportive friend. Cultivating gratitude trains your mind to notice and cherish the positive moments, helping to counteract the tendency to focus on the negative.

Incorporate these strategies into your journey of self-discovery and positive transformation. Remember, changing thinking patterns is a gradual process that requires patience and commitment. Just as a gardener tends to a garden, nurture your mind with these techniques, and watch as the landscape of your thoughts flourishes into one of positivity, resilience, and self-empowerment.

CBT for Anger Management

In the intricate landscape of human emotions, anger emerges as a powerful wave that can disrupt our sense of inner calm. However, what if there were a way to harness this intense emotion and transform it into a manageable force? This is where the brilliance of Cognitive Behavioral Therapy (CBT) comes into play, offering invaluable guidance to individuals seeking effective strategies for navigating and controlling their anger.

Anger, a universal human emotion, can be triggered by a variety of circumstances, from unmet expectations to perceived injustices or feelings of powerlessness.

Although a natural reaction, unmanaged anger can lead to destructive behaviors, strained relationships, and even impact our overall health.

The essence of CBT lies in its systematic approach to managing anger. This therapeutic framework acknowledges the intricate interplay between thoughts, emotions, and actions. By reshaping negative thought patterns, individuals can effectively alter their emotional responses and subsequent behaviors, enabling them to regain control over their anger.

Imagine possessing the ability to identify the sparks that ignite your anger – a unique power that CBT helps cultivate. This approach encourages individuals to become attuned to specific situations, thoughts, or feelings that trigger their emotional response. This heightened awareness empowers individuals to intercept the automatic reactions that typically follow, allowing for a more measured response.

A fundamental component of CBT involves challenging the validity of beliefs during anger-inducing episodes. Like a detective scrutinizing evidence, individuals are prompted to critically assess their beliefs. By questioning thoughts such as "Is this interpretation accurate?" or "Are there alternative explanations?" a more rational perspective can emerge, effectively counteracting the intensity of emotional reactions.

Another facet of CBT involves reshaping thought patterns linked to anger. The goal is to replace self-defeating thoughts with balanced and constructive alternatives. For instance, transforming "This situation is unbearable" into "This situation is challenging, but I possess the capacity to overcome it".

Within the realm of CBT lies a comprehensive toolkit of coping mechanisms, designed to dissipate the flames of anger. Imagine having an array of techniques at your disposal – from deep breathing exercises that soothe the nervous system to stepping away momentarily to recalibrate emotions. As these strategies are refined, individuals enhance their ability to respond to triggers in a composed and controlled manner.

Effective communication serves as a cornerstone for managing anger. CBT emphasizes assertive communication as a viable alternative to both aggressive and passive reactions. By articulating feelings and needs with respect and clarity, individuals lay the foundation for understanding and resolution, fostering healthier relationships.

CBT introduces relaxation techniques as anchors in the storm of anger. These techniques, spanning from progressive muscle relaxation to mindfulness meditation, equip individuals with the tools needed to navigate the tumultuous waters of anger with grace and clarity.

A critical aspect of CBT is consistent self-monitoring. Maintaining an anger journal provides insights into patterns, triggers, and the effectiveness of coping strategies. This heightened self-awareness expedites the journey toward improved anger management.

As you embark on the transformative journey of CBT for anger management, envision yourself as a skilled craftsman weaving a tapestry of emotional resilience. With each technique embraced, you weave a strand of self-awareness, a thread of patience, and a motif of emotional intelligence. Through dedication and practice, anger can evolve from a raging fire into a controlled flame – a force for personal growth and positive transformation.

3 CBT Techniques to Manage Anxiety and Work Stress

In today's fast-paced world, the pressures of work and daily life frequently lead to the emergence of anxiety and stress. The constant balancing of responsibilities often leaves us overwhelmed and mentally drained. However, within this tumultuous scenario, there exists a glimmer of hope – Cognitive Behavioral Therapy (CBT). This paragraph offers practical strategies that empower individuals, irrespective of their psychological background, to effectively navigate the realm of anxiety and work-induced stress with renewed strength and self-assuredness.

These are strategies that we have previously described in general terms, and which can be very effective when applied to stress management. Let us review them one by one, applied this time to anxiety control.

* * *

Technique 1: Cognitive Restructuring

Imagine possessing the ability to rewire your thought patterns, diminishing the grip of anxiety. This is the essence of cognitive restructuring, a foundational technique within Cognitive Behavioral Therapy (CBT). We have already talked about it at page __. At its core, cognitive restructuring entails recognizing distorted or irrational thoughts and challenging their validity. By replacing these negative thoughts with more balanced and rational alternatives, individuals can alleviate the intensity of anxiety.

This process involves becoming a detective of your own mind, critically examining the evidence for and against your anxious thoughts. By questioning the accuracy of these thoughts and considering alternative explanations, you can gain a more rational perspective. For instance, transforming the thought "I'll never be able to handle this workload" into "I have successfully managed challenging tasks in the past" can significantly diminish anxiety's impact.

Through consistent practice, cognitive restructuring equips individuals with the tools to confront and manage anxious thoughts effectively. By altering thought patterns, anxiety's power is diminished, allowing for greater emotional well-being and a more balanced outlook on life.

* * *

Technique 2: Exposure Therapy

Imagine facing your fears head-on, gradually diminishing their power over you. This is the essence of Exposure Therapy, a pivotal technique within Cognitive Behavioral Therapy (CBT). Exposure Therapy functions on the principle of systematically confronting anxiety-inducing situations to reduce their impact over time. By gradually exposing yourself to triggers in a controlled manner, you desensitize your response, ultimately diminishing the intensity of anxiety.

This technique embodies the adage "facing your fears". Suppose public speaking triggers anxiety. Through Exposure Therapy, you might start by speaking in front of a small group of friends or colleagues. As you build confidence, gradually progress to larger audiences. This process reshapes your brain's response to anxiety-inducing situations, allowing you to approach them with greater ease.

The rationale behind Exposure Therapy lies in habituation. Similar to how repeated exposure to a scent lessens its potency, repeated exposure to anxiety-inducing situations reduces their impact. By confronting these situations incrementally, you train your brain to develop a more balanced and rational response.

This technique is not about diving headlong into overwhelming situations but rather engaging in a gradual, controlled process. Exposure Therapy equips you with the skills to navigate anxiety-inducing scenarios with increased composure and reduced distress. It's a journey that empowers you to take charge of your anxiety and work-related stress, ultimately enhancing your overall well-being.

By consistently practicing Exposure Therapy, you cultivate resilience and a newfound sense of control over your anxieties. It's a testament to the transformative potential of CBT techniques in managing anxiety and stress, offering you a path towards reclaiming your inner calm and facing life's challenges with increased confidence.

* * *

Technique 3: Mindfulness Meditation

Picture finding solace amidst the storm, anchoring yourself in the present moment to navigate anxiety and stress. This is the essence of Mindfulness Meditation, a fundamental technique within Cognitive Behavioral Therapy (CBT). Mindfulness involves cultivating awareness of your thoughts, emotions, and sensations without judgment. By practicing mindfulness, you create a mental space that allows you to observe your thoughts without being consumed by them.

Mindfulness Meditation encourages you to tune into the sensations of your body and the rhythm of your breath. As you focus your attention on the present, you detach from the whirlwind of anxious thoughts. By observing these thoughts with detachment, you begin to recognize their transient nature – they come and go like waves in the ocean.

The practice of mindfulness teaches you to respond rather than react to anxiety. Instead of succumbing to the immediate impulse of anxiety, you learn to pause, observe, and then choose your response consciously. This shift from automatic reactions to intentional responses empowers you to manage anxiety and stress more effectively.

Research supports the efficacy of Mindfulness Meditation in reducing anxiety and enhancing emotional well-being. Studies have shown that regular mindfulness practice rewires the brain, leading to increased emotional regulation and decreased reactivity to stressors. The ability to remain centered in the present moment translates to greater control over anxious thoughts and a heightened sense of inner peace.

Incorporating mindfulness into your daily routine is a gradual process. Begin with short sessions, gradually extending them as you become more comfortable. By integrating mindfulness into your life, you forge a powerful tool that enables you to approach challenges with clarity and calmness. This technique, combined with the other CBT strategies, forms a holistic approach to managing anxiety and work-related stress.

As you immerse yourself in the practice of Mindfulness Meditation, you develop a deeper connection to the present moment. This connection becomes a sanctuary amidst the chaos, allowing you to navigate anxiety and stress with resilience and grace. It's a journey of self-discovery that empowers you to rewrite your relationship with anxiety, fostering a greater sense of equilibrium and well-being.

* * *

Sources of Strength: Evidence and Guidance

The integration of thought restructuring, exposure therapy, and mindfulness meditation forms a comprehensive toolkit for managing anxiety.

Research underscores the validity of CBT's techniques. Studies have demonstrated their efficacy in reducing anxiety symptoms and enhancing individuals' overall well-being. The National Institute of Mental Health recognizes CBT as a first-line treatment for anxiety disorders, affirming its credibility in the psychological community.

Guided by reputable psychologists and supported by empirical research, CBT techniques provide individuals with concrete strategies to manage their anxiety and work stress. By learning to reframe thoughts, confront fears gradually, and embrace mindfulness, individuals gain the tools to navigate the challenges of modern life with resilience.

In this journey of transformation, individuals tap into a wellspring of psychological wisdom that enables them to shift their relationship with anxiety. As you immerse yourself in the techniques of CBT, you stand on the shoulders of psychological giants and harness the power of evidence-backed strategies.

CBT for Eating Disorders: Navigating a Path to Recovery

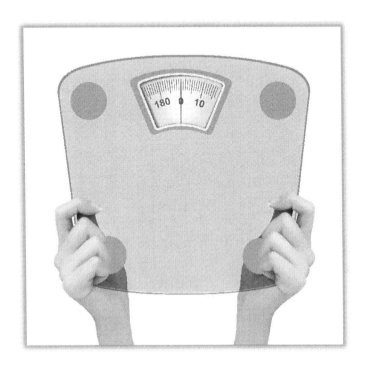

In a world that often fixates on appearance and body ideals, the battle against eating disorders can be an arduous one. The complexities of these disorders extend far beyond the surface, intertwining with emotions, self-perception, and mental well-being. In this section we will explore how Cognitive Behavioral Therapy (CBT) serves as a guiding light for individuals seeking a way out of the labyrinth of eating disorders. This guide, aimed at a non-expert audience, is a beacon of hope, offering insights and strategies to foster a healthier relationship with food, body image, and self-esteem.

Eating disorders encompass a spectrum of conditions, including anorexia nervosa, bulimia nervosa, and binge-eating disorder. These disorders are often fueled by distorted beliefs about body image and an unhealthy preoccupation with food and weight. The realm of CBT offers a holistic approach, addressing the intricate connections between thoughts, emotions, and behaviors that underpin these disorders.

CBT for eating disorders involves a multifaceted approach, starting with the identification of negative thought patterns. Individuals are encouraged to recognize and challenge distorted beliefs about their body, weight, and self-worth. By critically evaluating these beliefs and introducing alternative perspectives, CBT lays the groundwork for dismantling the foundation of eating disorders.

One hallmark of CBT is its emphasis on self-monitoring. Keeping a diary of thoughts, emotions, and eating behaviors provides individuals with valuable insights into triggers and patterns. This self-awareness serves as a compass, guiding individuals towards healthier choices and helping them identify moments when negative thought patterns emerge.

The process of cognitive restructuring plays a pivotal role in CBT for eating disorders. By replacing self-defeating thoughts with rational and balanced alternatives, individuals can cultivate a healthier self-perception. For instance, shifting from "I must be thin to be valuable" to "My worth is not determined by my appearance" fosters a more positive relationship with oneself.

Moreover, CBT addresses behavioral aspects of eating disorders. It equips individuals with coping strategies to manage impulses and urges related to food. By introducing healthy coping mechanisms, individuals learn to navigate stressors and emotions without resorting to disordered eating behaviors.

Family involvement often plays a crucial role in CBT for eating disorders, acknowledging the impact of the support system. Sessions may include family members to foster open communication, understanding, and the development of strategies to create a conducive environment for recovery.

The journey to recovery from eating disorders is a challenging one, but CBT offers a roadmap toward healing. By integrating thought restructuring, behavioral strategies, and family involvement, individuals gradually reconstruct their relationship with food and their bodies.

Research underscores the effectiveness of CBT in treating eating disorders. Numerous studies highlight its positive impact on reducing binge-eating episodes, promoting weight stability, and improving overall well-being. The National Eating Disorders Association acknowledges CBT as a prominent therapeutic approach, lending credibility to its significance in the field.

As individuals tread the path of CBT for eating disorders, they not only address disordered eating patterns but also embark on a journey of self-discovery and empowerment. By challenging distorted beliefs, adopting healthier coping mechanisms, and fostering self-compassion, individuals can navigate the complexities of eating disorders with renewed strength and the promise of a healthier future.

How to Apply CBT Techniques to Any Other Mental Health and Stress-Related Disorder

In the intricate tapestry of human experience, mental health and stress-related disorders are threads that can weave through our lives, affecting our emotional well-being and overall quality of life. While the challenges these disorders pose can be overwhelming, there exists a guiding compass – Cognitive Behavioral Therapy (CBT). CBT serves as a versatile toolkit, offering strategies that individuals from any psychological background can employ to navigate the labyrinth of mental health and stress-related struggles with resilience and empowerment.

Mental health and stress-related disorders encompass a wide spectrum, including anxiety disorders, depression, post-traumatic stress disorder (PTSD), and more. The common thread among these conditions is the interplay of thoughts, emotions, and behaviors that can exacerbate distress. CBT, a cornerstone in psychological therapy, offers an approach that can be tailored to address the unique challenges of each disorder.

For individuals with anxiety disorders, CBT helps them confront and manage irrational fears through exposure therapy and cognitive restructuring. Depression, characterized by a cycle of negative thinking, responds well to CBT's methods of challenging distorted beliefs and fostering a more positive self-perception.

CBT can be particularly effective in addressing the aftermath of traumatic experiences. In cases of PTSD, it helps individuals process and reframe traumatic memories, reducing the intensity of flashbacks and triggers. By modifying the associations linked to traumatic events, individuals regain a sense of control over their emotional responses.

The principles of CBT extend to stress-related disorders as well. Chronic stress can manifest in various forms, impacting physical health and emotional well-being. CBT equips individuals with coping strategies to manage stressors, enhance resilience, and cultivate a balanced approach to life's challenges.

Family involvement and interpersonal relationships are also pivotal aspects of CBT's application. By enhancing communication skills and fostering understanding within relationships, individuals can create a supportive environment that complements their journey toward healing.

The versatility of CBT techniques extends beyond therapeutic settings. They can be seamlessly integrated into daily life, offering individuals the means to confront and manage distressing thoughts and emotions as they arise. By practicing mindfulness, thought reframing, and relaxation techniques, individuals arm themselves with tools that foster emotional regulation and well-being.

Research consistently supports the effectiveness of CBT in addressing a range of mental health and stress-related disorders. Clinical studies demonstrate its positive impact on reducing symptoms and improving overall functioning. The endorsement of reputable organizations, such as the American Psychological Association, further reinforces CBT's significance in the field of mental health.

As you embark on the journey of applying CBT techniques to mental health and stress-related challenges, envision yourself as an artist wielding a palette of resilience and self-awareness. With each stroke of thought restructuring, each brush of coping strategy, you paint a canvas of empowerment and growth.

Relapse Prevention: Sustaining Progress Beyond Therapy

Knowing how to manage possible relapses is as important as the therapy itself.

In the complex labyrinth of personal growth and transformation, the journey doesn't end with the completion of therapy. While therapy equips individuals with essential tools and insights, the real challenge lies in maintaining the progress achieved and preventing relapse. This is where the concept of relapse prevention takes center stage, offering a vital roadmap to ensure that the strides made during therapy are sustained in the long run. This book is also intended to teach individuals, even those without prior psychological expertise, how to fortify their emotional resilience and safeguard their hard-earned progress.

Imagine the journey of personal growth as a marathon rather than a sprint. Just as athletes train rigorously to maintain their peak performance, individuals transitioning from therapy must cultivate strategies to navigate life's challenges without losing the ground they've gained.

Relapse, in the context of mental health, refers to a recurrence of symptoms or setbacks after a period of improvement. It's important to acknowledge that setbacks are a natural part of the journey, but they can be minimized through relapse prevention strategies.

One of the cornerstones of relapse prevention is self-awareness. This involves recognizing early warning signs and triggers that might signal a potential relapse. By being attuned to shifts in thoughts, emotions, and behaviors, individuals can intervene before minor setbacks escalate.

The practice of mindfulness, a technique often introduced in therapy, becomes invaluable in relapse prevention. Mindfulness cultivates present-moment awareness and acceptance, allowing individuals to navigate challenges with a clear and grounded perspective. It becomes a compass that guides them away from the patterns that once led to distress.

Support networks play a pivotal role in relapse prevention. Family, friends, or support groups provide a safety net of understanding and encouragement. By fostering open communication, individuals can seek assistance and share their challenges without judgment.

Thanks to Cognitive Behavioral Therapy (CBT) teachings and techniques, individuals are equipped with skills to identify and challenge negative thought patterns that might trigger a relapse. This ongoing process of thought restructuring empowers individuals to navigate setbacks with resilience.

Creating a personalized relapse prevention plan is crucial. This plan outlines individual triggers, coping strategies, and steps to take in case of a relapse. Having a concrete roadmap in place enhances the sense of control and preparedness.

It's important to remember that relapse is not synonymous with failure. It's a detour on the path of progress, one that can be navigated with self-compassion and a commitment to change. Each setback offers an opportunity for growth and learning, a chance to reinforce the strategies that lead to emotional well-being.

Research supports the effectiveness of relapse prevention strategies. Studies show that individuals who engage in these strategies are better equipped to manage stressors and setbacks, leading to improved overall well-being.

As individuals embark on the journey of relapse prevention, they embrace the notion that personal growth is a continuous process. Just as a gardener tends to a delicate plant, nurturing its growth and protecting it from adverse conditions, individuals tend to their emotional well-being with diligence and care.

The completion of therapy marks the commencement of a new chapter – one characterized by the commitment to preserving the progress made. Relapse prevention is the compass that guides individuals towards lasting transformation, a testament to their strength and resilience. As you navigate this phase, envision yourself as a guardian of your emotional well-being, equipped with the tools to thrive even in the face of challenges.

EXPLORING ALTERNATIVE THERAPIES TO COMPLEMENT YOUR WELL-BEING JOURNEY

In the realm of mental health and wellness, individuals are presented with a diverse array of approaches that extend beyond the scope of traditional Cognitive Behavioral Therapy (CBT). While CBT is a well-established and evidence-based framework, it's important to recognize that different paths resonate with different people.

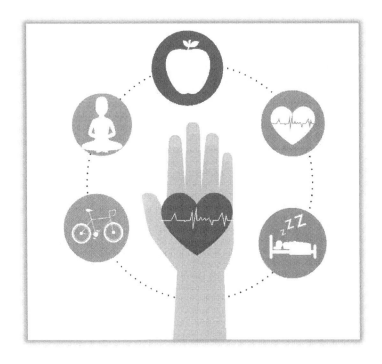

Psychotherapy and/or medications

In the intricate landscape of mental health care, individuals are presented with a dual avenue to address their psychological well-being – psychotherapy and medications. These two approaches, while distinct, often intertwine in comprehensive treatment plans, catering to the diverse needs and complexities of individuals' conditions. As we delve into the realm of psychotherapy and medications, we uncover the nuances of each approach and explore their collaborative potential in fostering mental wellness.

* * *

The Essence of Psychotherapy

Psychotherapy, often referred to as "talk therapy", encompasses a range of therapeutic modalities designed to address various mental health concerns. The fundamental premise is to provide individuals with a safe and supportive environment to explore their emotions, thoughts, and behaviors. Through guided conversations, psychotherapy aims to unravel the underlying causes of distress, enhance self-awareness, and develop effective coping strategies.

Numerous forms of psychotherapy exist, each tailored to specific conditions and individual preferences. Cognitive Behavioral Therapy (CBT), for instance, focuses on identifying and modifying negative thought patterns, while Dialectical Behavior Therapy (DBT) helps individuals regulate emotions and improve interpersonal relationships. Other approaches, such as Psychodynamic Therapy and Humanistic Therapy, delve into deeper layers of the psyche and the exploration of the self.

* * *

The Role of Medications

Medications, on the other hand, offer a pharmacological route to managing mental health conditions. Often prescribed by medical professionals, medications can help alleviate symptoms by targeting physiological imbalances in neurotransmitters – the chemical messengers in the brain. For instance, antidepressants are commonly prescribed to alleviate symptoms of depression and anxiety by affecting serotonin levels. Antipsychotic medications, on the other hand, are used to manage symptoms of conditions like schizophrenia.

The decision to incorporate medications into a treatment plan is a nuanced one, involving discussions between individuals and their healthcare providers. Factors such as the nature and severity of the condition, past treatment responses, and potential side effects are all considered. Medications can provide much-needed relief, especially when symptoms are severe or chronic.

* * *

The Synergy of a Dual Approach

While psychotherapy and medications are distinct modalities, they often complement each other in a dual approach. This synergy is particularly evident in cases where conditions are complex and multifaceted. For instance, individuals with depression might benefit from a combination of antidepressant medications and CBT. Medications can alleviate acute symptoms, enabling individuals to engage more effectively in therapy and implement coping strategies. On the other hand, psychotherapy provides the tools to address underlying thought patterns and behaviors, contributing to long-term recovery.

It is important to note that the choice between psychotherapy and medications is not mutually exclusive. Rather, it's a collaborative decision informed by the individual's preferences, the nature of the condition, and the expertise of mental health professionals. A well-informed and open dialogue between individuals and their healthcare providers forms the foundation for effective treatment planning.

* * *

An Individualized Path to Healing

In the journey toward mental wellness, the dual approach of psychotherapy and medications reflects the diverse spectrum of human experiences. Just as no two individuals are alike, their mental health journeys are equally unique. Some may find solace and progress through psychotherapy alone, while others may benefit from a combination of therapy and medications. The key lies in recognizing that there is no one-size-fits-all solution – only a tailored approach that honors each individual's needs, preferences, and aspirations.

In this path of self-care, envision yourself as an architect of your own well-being. Your journey is marked by collaboration, introspection, and the empowerment to make informed decisions that pave the way toward emotional vitality and resilience. Through this journey, you can harness the power of both psychotherapy and medications to create a comprehensive strategy for nurturing your mental health and reclaiming your sense of equilibrium.

Meditation practices

In the fast-paced rhythm of our contemporary lives, the quest for inner serenity and emotional equilibrium has become a paramount concern. Amid the bustling world and the demands of daily routines, the allure of meditation practices beckons as a sanctuary for the mind, offering respite from the cacophony and a chance to cultivate mindfulness and tranquility. This chapter embarks on a voyage of discovery into the realm of meditation practices, delving into their nuances, benefits, and potential impact on our mental well-being.

Meditation, with its ancient roots intertwined across cultures and traditions, has transcended its spiritual origins to become a scientifically validated method for enhancing mental and emotional health. It encompasses a spectrum of techniques, all of which share the common thread of turning the gaze inward and embracing the present moment with conscious awareness.

At the heart of meditation practices lies mindfulness meditation, which beckons practitioners to be fully present and aware of their thoughts, sensations, and emotions without judgment. Rooted in Buddhist traditions, mindfulness has gained prominence as a tool for stress reduction and emotional regulation. Studies have shown that regular mindfulness practice can alleviate symptoms of anxiety, depression, and stress, while also promoting self-awareness and emotional balance.

Guided imagery meditation, an intriguing practice, harnesses the mind's imaginative power to evoke feelings of relaxation and well-being. By conjuring vivid mental images, individuals are transported to serene landscapes or scenarios that nurture positive emotions. This technique has been employed in various contexts, from managing stress to enhancing performance in sports and the arts.

Transcendental Meditation (TM), emerging from Vedic traditions, revolves around the repetition of a specific mantra. This mantra serves as a vehicle to transcend ordinary thought patterns, inviting practitioners to delve into deeper states of consciousness. Research suggests that TM may contribute to reduced anxiety, enhanced cognitive function, and increased overall resilience to stress.

Loving-kindness meditation, known as Metta meditation, centers on cultivating feelings of compassion and goodwill toward oneself and others. This practice involves the repetition of affirmations or phrases that radiate kindness and empathy. Scientific exploration into loving-kindness meditation has unveiled its potential to increase feelings of interconnectedness, diminish negative emotions, and foster a positive self-concept.

Venturing into the realm of meditation requires a balanced blend of curiosity, commitment, and patience. The benefits of meditation extend far beyond a mere escape from the chaos of life. Through consistent practice, meditation equips individuals with life skills that resonate throughout their daily experiences. The ability to anchor oneself in the present moment, respond to challenges with equanimity, and foster a sense of inner peace become integral aspects of a well-nurtured mind.

As you embark on your meditation journey, consider yourself a curious traveler exploring the vast landscapes of your own consciousness. Patience and persistence are essential companions, as meditation is a skill cultivated over time. Commence with brief sessions, gradually extending their duration as you become more attuned to the practice.

Incorporating meditation into your daily routine doesn't necessitate elaborate rituals. A quiet space, a comfortable posture, and a focused mind are all you need to begin. Whether you choose mindfulness, guided imagery, Transcendental Meditation, or loving-kindness as your vehicle, the essence lies in consistent practice and an open-hearted approach.

Amid the ebb and flow of life's challenges, meditation emerges as a compass that guides you to an inner sanctuary of calm. Embrace the opportunity to partake in an ancient tradition that bridges cultures and eras. As you journey inward, remember that you are treading a path that countless seekers have walked before you. This voyage symbolizes your commitment to nurturing your mental well-being and embracing the boundless potential residing within your own mind.

Lifestyle changes such as exercising, relaxing, and eating healthier

In the ever-evolving landscape of well-being, the intersection of mental health and lifestyle choices takes center stage. Amid the intricate dance of daily life, simple yet profound changes in habits and routines can wield a transformative impact on mental and emotional equilibrium. This chapter embarks on an exploration of lifestyle changes – encompassing exercise, relaxation, and dietary choices – and their pivotal role in fostering mental well-being.

Physical activity, often considered a cornerstone of a healthy lifestyle, extends its influence beyond physical fitness. Regular exercise triggers the release of endorphins, the body's natural mood enhancers, contributing to reduced stress, anxiety, and depression. Engaging in activities that elevate heart rate not only promotes cardiovascular health but also nurtures cognitive function and emotional resilience.

The synergy between exercise and mental well-being is rooted in biological mechanisms. Physical exertion stimulates the production of brain-derived neurotrophic factor (BDNF), a protein associated with improved cognitive function and enhanced mood regulation. From brisk walks to yoga sessions, the spectrum of activities offers a canvas for individuals to paint their paths to emotional harmony.

Relaxation, often neglected in the hustle and bustle of life, emerges as a potent tool for reducing stress and enhancing mental clarity. Techniques such as progressive muscle relaxation, deep breathing exercises, and guided imagery provide solace amidst the storm of daily demands. By carving out moments for relaxation, individuals create sanctuaries of calm that serve as buffers against stressors.

Mindful relaxation, which invites individuals to immerse themselves fully in the present moment, infuses a sense of tranquility into daily routines. Mindfulness practices, when incorporated into relaxation techniques, elevate their efficacy by fostering a heightened awareness of bodily sensations, emotions, and thoughts. The result is an enhanced ability to manage stressors and cultivate emotional resilience.

Diet, a realm traditionally associated with physical health, unveils its far-reaching impact on mental well-being. Emerging research highlights the gut-brain connection, underscoring how dietary choices can influence mood and cognitive function. A diet rich in whole foods, antioxidants, and omega-3 fatty acids is linked to improved mental health outcomes.

Sugar-laden diets, often accompanied by processed foods, may contribute to inflammation and oxidative stress, potentially exacerbating symptoms of anxiety and depression. Incorporating nutrient-dense foods, such as leafy greens, berries, and nuts, can supply the brain with essential vitamins and minerals that support emotional well-being.

The role of hydration in mental health is often underestimated. Dehydration can lead to cognitive impairments and mood disturbances. Ensuring adequate water intake is a simple yet effective strategy to maintain cognitive function and emotional balance.

As you embark on the journey of integrating lifestyle changes into your routine, remember that small shifts can yield significant transformations. Consider setting achievable goals, such as taking a daily walk, dedicating time for relaxation, or embracing nutrient-rich foods. The essence lies in consistency and a gentle approach. The goal is not perfection but a sustainable lifestyle that nurtures your mental and emotional health.

The interplay between exercise, relaxation, and dietary choices forms the foundation of a holistic approach to mental well-being. These lifestyle changes are interconnected threads woven into the fabric of your daily life. By nurturing your physical body, you create a resilient vessel that supports your emotional and cognitive realms. Embrace the journey with open arms, knowing that each step toward well-being is an investment in your holistic health.

Other Options

In the quest for holistic well-being, a spectrum of approaches beckons beyond conventional methods. While psychotherapy, medications, meditation, exercise, and dietary adjustments form the pillars of mental health support, an array of alternative options shines as potential avenues for cultivating emotional balance and resilience. This chapter embarks on an exploration of these unique strategies, from the enchanting practice of forest bathing to the soothing embrace of pet therapy and the expressive canvas of art therapy.

* * *

Forest Bathing: Nurturing the Soul Amidst Nature's Embrace

Imagine immersing yourself in a tranquil forest, allowing the symphony of rustling leaves and chirping birds to envelop you. This practice, known as forest bathing or Shinrin yoku, emanates from Japanese culture and is renowned for its therapeutic effects. Studies highlight its potential to reduce stress hormones, lower blood pressure, and enhance mood. The healing power of nature, combined with mindful presence, creates a harmonious sanctuary for emotional restoration.

* * *

Pet Therapy: Unconditional Love in Furry Form

The companionship of animals transcends words, offering solace, empathy, and non-judgmental support. Pet therapy, scientifically referred to as animal-assisted therapy, involves trained animals that provide comfort and affection. Interacting with pets triggers the release of oxytocin, the "love hormone", which fosters a sense of well-being. From dogs to cats, and even horses, these animal allies forge connections that extend beyond words, providing emotional refuge.

* * *

Art Therapy: Expressive Liberation for the Mind and Soul

The canvas becomes a mirror of emotions, and colors dance as language for the soul in art therapy. This approach harnesses the creative process to explore, express, and process emotions. Individuals channel their innermost feelings onto paper, canvas, or other mediums. The act of creation allows for the release of pent-up emotions, unveiling insights and promoting self-awareness. Through colors, shapes, and strokes, individuals navigate their internal landscapes, finding empowerment in their artistic expressions.

* * *

Dance/Movement Therapy: The Language of the Body

Movement is a vessel through which emotions flow, and dance/movement therapy captures this essence. Guided by trained therapists, individuals express themselves through movement, freeing themselves from inhibitions and fostering emotional release. The body's language becomes a conduit for processing feelings that words might struggle to articulate. Through dance, individuals tap into the wisdom of their bodies, unearthing emotions and connecting with their inner selves.

* * *

Music Therapy: Harmonizing the Mind and Spirit

Music carries the power to evoke emotions, trigger memories, and create a sense of connection. Music therapy employs this auditory magic to address mental health challenges. Whether through playing instruments, singing, or simply listening to music, individuals find solace and a channel for expression. Music therapy can alleviate symptoms of anxiety, depression, and trauma, providing a safe space for emotional exploration.

* * *

Equine-Assisted Therapy: Forming Bonds with Majestic Allies

In the realm of unconventional therapies, equine-assisted therapy stands out. Interacting with horses under the guidance of therapists fosters metaphorical experiences that reflect real-life challenges. These interactions nurture skills such as communication, assertiveness, and trust-building. The majestic presence of horses creates a unique arena for self-discovery and personal growth.

As you embark on your journey toward mental well-being, remember that the path is as diverse as the human experience. Exploring alternative approaches offers an opportunity to discover what resonates with you on a profound level. These unconventional avenues, whether it's the soothing embrace of a forest, the wagging tail of a furry friend, the strokes of a paintbrush, the rhythm of dance, or the melodies of music, can become tools for emotional empowerment. Consider embracing the richness of these alternative options as you forge your unique path toward holistic wellness.

As you navigate the chapters of your life, you possess the agency to weave together a tapestry of well-being that draws from an array of strategies. The beauty lies in the blend, the fusion of conventional and alternative approaches, creating a symphony of support that resonates with your unique essence. As you continue your journey, remember that each choice you make, whether traditional or unconventional, is a step toward nurturing your mental and emotional health.

BONUS EXTRA

TOP 10 MOST FREQUENTLY ASKED QUESTIONS ON CBT

There are a lot of questions on CBT on social media and online forum.

We have already answered to some of the questions in this book.

Here below you can find answers to the Top 10 Most Frequently Asked Questions on CBT

1) Is CBT (cognitive behavioral therapy) outdated?

Cognitive Behavioral Therapy (CBT) stands as a beacon of effectiveness and relevance in the ever-evolving landscape of mental health treatment. While newer therapeutic approaches have emerged, CBT remains a stalwart contender, fortified by a rich history of empirical support, practical applicability, adaptability, and resonance with modern challenges.

The notion that CBT is outdated is far from accurate. Its enduring prominence is rooted in its robust empirical foundation. Decades of research studies and clinical trials have consistently demonstrated CBT's efficacy in treating a wide array of psychological disorders. From anxiety and depression to phobias and post-traumatic stress disorder (PTSD), CBT has consistently showcased its effectiveness. This evidence-based approach ensures that CBT's techniques are not mere conjecture, but rather a rigorously tested and refined toolkit for mental well-being.

A key facet of CBT's staying power is its practicality and accessibility.

CBT equips individuals with tangible skills and strategies that can be immediately applied to their daily lives. This down-to-earth nature sets it apart from more abstract therapeutic modalities and resonates deeply with individuals seeking actionable solutions. By zeroing in on the present moment, CBT assists individuals in identifying and challenging negative thought patterns that fuel distressing emotions and behaviors. This hands-on involvement empowers individuals to take an active role in managing their mental health journey, enhancing their sense of agency and self-efficacy.

In the ever-accelerating digital age, CBT has seamlessly adapted to meet modern needs. Technological advancements have facilitated the integration of CBT techniques into online platforms, mobile applications, and telehealth services. This evolution has democratized access to effective mental health care, making it available to individuals who may face geographical, logistical, or time-related barriers. CBT's accessibility is no longer limited by physical proximity to a therapist's office; instead, it can be accessed at one's convenience, fostering a more inclusive and accommodating therapeutic landscape.

Moreover, CBT's resilience lies in its inherent flexibility. While its foundational principles remain steadfast, CBT has demonstrated an impressive ability to integrate with and enhance other therapeutic modalities. It has synergistically fused with mindfulness practices, acceptance and commitment therapy (ACT), and dialectical behavior therapy (DBT), resulting in innovative hybrid approaches. This versatility enables therapists to tailor interventions to individual needs, ensuring that the therapeutic journey is uniquely attuned to the complexities of each person's experience.

In a world characterized by rapid change, the skills cultivated through CBT hold profound relevance. CBT equips individuals with the tools to navigate the complex web of stressors, uncertainties, and challenges that define modern existence. By fostering self-awareness, teaching problem-solving strategies, and promoting emotional regulation, CBT empowers individuals to effectively manage stress, enhance resilience, and optimize their mental well-being. In essence, CBT serves as a compass, guiding individuals through the maze of contemporary life and enabling them to emerge stronger and more equipped to thrive.

Beyond the realm of clinical therapy, CBT's influence extends into various domains. Its principles have been successfully integrated into education, business, and sports psychology. In educational settings, educators harness CBT techniques to foster emotional intelligence, enhance communication skills, and promote effective learning strategies. In the corporate world, professionals leverage CBT to manage workplace stress, enhance interpersonal dynamics, and foster a positive organizational culture. Athletes and performers utilize CBT to optimize their mental preparation, enhance focus, and manage performance anxiety. This far-reaching impact underscores the universal applicability of CBT's principles and techniques.

In a world where the concept of mental well-being has gained increasing recognition, CBT remains a cornerstone of effective mental health care. Its empirical grounding, practicality, adaptability, and resonance with modern challenges have solidified its status as a time-tested and enduring therapeutic approach. While the therapeutic landscape continues to evolve, CBT stands firm, a beacon of hope, and a trusted ally in the quest for mental health, personal growth, and holistic well-being. In embracing the principles of CBT, we embark on a profound journey of self-discovery, healing, and transformation—a journey that extends beyond the confines of this book, empowering us to navigate the complexities of life with newfound resilience and purpose.

2) Is Cognitive Behavioral Therapy an effective approach in treating Major Depression?

Cognitive Behavioral Therapy (CBT) continues to stand as a robust and effective approach to treating Major Depression, challenging any notions of being outdated. In fact, its enduring relevance and widespread acceptance stem from its solid foundation in psychological theory, its evidence-based nature, and its capacity to adapt to modern advancements in mental health care. To comprehend why CBT remains a cornerstone in treating Major Depression, one must delve into its principles, empirical support, and the dynamic ways it addresses the complexities of this debilitating condition.

CBT's effectiveness in treating Major Depression is rooted in its comprehensive framework that addresses the intricate interplay between thoughts, emotions, and behaviors. Rather than viewing the mind as a collection of isolated components, CBT recognizes the intricate connections between cognitive processes, emotional experiences, and behavioral patterns. This integrated approach is particularly well-suited for Major Depression, a disorder characterized by pervasive negative thought patterns, emotional distress, and withdrawal from activities.

Empirical evidence provides resounding support for the efficacy of CBT in treating Major Depression. Countless research studies, meta-analyses, and clinical trials consistently demonstrate its effectiveness in reducing depressive symptoms, preventing relapse, and enhancing overall well-being. These studies often compare CBT to other therapeutic modalities, placebo interventions, or pharmacological treatments, showcasing CBT's robust and enduring effects.

One of the distinguishing features of CBT is its adaptability. It has evolved over time to incorporate innovative strategies and techniques, making it a highly versatile approach in the contemporary landscape of mental health care. For instance, technology-assisted CBT, delivered through online platforms or mobile applications, has emerged as a convenient and effective option for individuals seeking treatment. This adaptability ensures that CBT remains accessible and relevant to individuals across diverse backgrounds and lifestyles.

CBT's core principles align seamlessly with the modern understanding of the neurobiology of Major Depression. It recognizes the neuroplasticity of the brain, emphasizing that new thought patterns and behaviors can reshape neural pathways and foster positive change. This alignment with neuroscientific insights lends further credibility to CBT's enduring efficacy.

In the context of Major Depression, CBT offers a structured and systematic approach to transforming maladaptive thought patterns. Individuals learn to identify and challenge negative automatic thoughts, which often contribute to the perpetuation of depressive symptoms. Through guided self-exploration and collaboration with a skilled therapist, individuals develop the ability to reframe their thinking and cultivate a more balanced and realistic perspective.

Moreover, CBT equips individuals with a diverse toolkit of coping skills. These skills extend beyond cognitive restructuring to encompass emotion regulation, mindfulness practices, and behavioral activation. This holistic approach acknowledges the multi-faceted nature of Major Depression and provides individuals with a comprehensive set of strategies to manage their symptoms and enhance their overall quality of life.

CBT's effectiveness is further magnified when combined with other therapeutic modalities or pharmacological interventions. Collaborative care models, where CBT is integrated with medication management, have shown particularly promising results in treating severe and chronic forms of Major Depression. This integration capitalizes on the synergistic benefits of addressing both psychological and biological aspects of the disorder.

As mental health care continues to evolve, CBT remains at the forefront due to its solid theoretical underpinnings, empirical validation, and adaptability. Its relevance is not merely a matter of historical significance; it is a testament to its capacity to continuously evolve and integrate contemporary scientific insights. CBT's ability to empower individuals with the skills to challenge negative thought patterns, regulate their emotions, and engage in adaptive behaviors positions it as a timeless and indispensable approach in the comprehensive treatment of Major Depression. In embracing the principles of CBT, individuals embark on a journey of healing, growth, and transformation, guided by a therapeutic approach that has stood the test of time and remains a beacon of hope for those navigating the challenges of Major Depression.

3) Can I perform Cognitive behavioral therapy on myself?

Yes, it is indeed possible to apply Cognitive Behavioral Therapy (CBT) techniques by yourself, making self-administered CBT a valuable tool for personal development and emotional well-being. CBT is built on the premise that our thoughts, emotions, and behaviors are interconnected, and altering negative thought patterns can positively influence our emotions and actions. While working with a professional therapist can provide specialized guidance and support, practicing CBT on your own can offer meaningful benefits.

Self-directed CBT involves understanding the fundamental principles of CBT and applying its techniques to your own thoughts and behaviors. It can be an effective way to address mild to moderate emotional challenges, improve coping skills, and foster a healthier mindset. You can engage in self-CBT by applying the strategies described in this book daily.

In conclusion, self-administered CBT can contribute to improving your mental well-being by empowering you to challenge negative thought patterns, modify behaviors, and enhance emotional regulation. With adequate self-awareness, education, and commitment, self-CBT can be a valuable aspect of your journey toward personal growth and improved emotional resilience.

However, it's important to acknowledge that while self-CBT can be effective for many individuals seeking personal growth and managing milder emotional concerns, it might not be suitable for severe mental health conditions or complex trauma. If you find that your challenges persist, your emotional well-being deteriorates, or you struggle to make progress on your own, seeking professional help is recommended.

4) How long does it take for cognitive behavioral therapy to work?

The timeline for when Cognitive Behavioral Therapy (CBT) starts to show results can vary widely based on individual factors, the nature of the issue being addressed, and the frequency of therapy sessions. Generally, CBT is considered a relatively short-term therapeutic approach compared to some other forms of psychotherapy.

Many individuals experience positive changes within a few weeks to a few months of consistent CBT sessions. Often, after about 12 to 20 sessions, individuals notice improvements in their thought patterns, emotions, and behaviors. However, this is a general guideline, and the speed of progress can be influenced by several factors:

- Condition Severity: The severity of the issue being treated plays a role. Mild to moderate concerns might show improvement more quickly, while severe conditions might require longer-term therapy.

- Commitment and Engagement: Active participation and commitment to practicing CBT techniques both during sessions and in daily life can expedite progress.

- Individual Differences: Each person's unique history, personality, and circumstances influence how they respond to therapy. Some individuals are quick to integrate new coping skills, while others might take more time.

- Consistency: Attending regular sessions and consistently applying learned techniques in daily life can accelerate the pace of improvement.

- Therapeutic Relationship: A positive and trusting relationship between you and your therapist can enhance the effectiveness of CBT.

- Complexity of the Issue: Addressing deeply ingrained thought patterns or complex issues might require more time to achieve lasting change.

- Aftercare and Maintenance: After the active phase of therapy, individuals often benefit from periodic "booster" sessions or continuing to apply learned skills to prevent relapse.

It's important to understand that CBT equips you with tools for lifelong personal growth and effective coping, even beyond the structured therapy period. Just as you continue to maintain physical health with exercise, mental well-being benefits from ongoing mental exercises.

In summary, while there is no fixed duration for CBT to work, many individuals start experiencing positive changes within a few months of consistent practice. The collaborative effort between you and your therapist, combined with your engagement and dedication, significantly influences the pace of progress. It's crucial to have realistic expectations and understand that CBT is an investment in your long-term well-being that extends beyond the therapy room.

5) In which cases would cognitive-behavioral therapy be a bad choice?

Cognitive Behavioral Therapy (CBT) is an adaptive and empirically supported therapeutic approach that has gained significant recognition for its effectiveness in treating a diverse array of mental health conditions. Its reputation for success is well-deserved, yet it's crucial to acknowledge that no single therapeutic method can be universally applied to all individuals and situations. Within the dynamic landscape of mental health care, there are instances where

CBT may not emerge as the optimal or most effective choice, underscoring the importance of considering individual circumstances and tailoring interventions accordingly.

One noteworthy context where CBT might not serve as the primary approach is when addressing severe and complex mental illnesses, such as schizophrenia or bipolar disorder. These intricate conditions necessitate a multifaceted treatment strategy that encompasses medication management, psychoeducation, and specialized therapies. While CBT can certainly play a valuable role as an adjunctive tool for addressing specific symptoms or challenges, it may not be the cornerstone of intervention required to manage the multifaceted nature of these disorders comprehensively.

Another pivotal consideration revolves around the individual's level of motivation and active participation in therapy. CBT is characterized by its collaborative and skill-building nature, demanding proactive engagement from the client. If an individual lacks the willingness or capacity to partake in therapeutic exercises, complete assigned tasks, or apply learned techniques outside the therapeutic setting, the full potential of CBT may remain unrealized.

In the field of complex trauma, CBT might not adequately address all facets of therapeutic needs. Individuals grappling with complex trauma or dissociative disorders could derive greater benefit from trauma-focused modalities like Eye Movement Desensitization and Reprocessing (EMDR) or Dialectical Behavior Therapy (DBT), both of which offer specialized techniques tailored to address trauma-related symptoms and dissociation.

Cultural and linguistic factors can exert a profound influence on the therapeutic process, potentially impeding effective communication and mutual understanding between the client and therapist. In scenarios characterized by significant cultural disparities or language barriers, the presence of a culturally sensitive therapist proficient in the client's language becomes pivotal for establishing a productive therapeutic relationship.

Furthermore, the intricate nature of CBT, which heavily emphasizes cognitive restructuring and the application of cognitive and behavioral techniques, might prove challenging for individuals with profound intellectual disabilities or cognitive impairments. In such cases, alternative therapeutic modalities centered on sensory experiences or creative expression may offer a more accessible and effective avenue for therapeutic growth.

The establishment of a robust therapeutic alliance is fundamental to the success of any therapeutic approach, including CBT. Instances where the client and therapist struggle to establish a positive and trusting relationship may impede the efficacy of CBT. Exploring alternative therapeutic models or considering the possibility of working with a different therapist who better aligns with the client's needs could be advantageous.

For individuals seeking a more introspective and emotionally exploratory therapeutic experience, the pragmatic and solution-focused nature of CBT might not fully resonate with their aspirations. Psychodynamic or person-centered therapies, which delve deeper into emotional experiences and the therapeutic relationship, could offer a more suitable framework for addressing their unique requirements.

Certain medical conditions, such as severe substance use disorders or neurological impairments, have the potential to influence an individual's capacity to fully engage in CBT. Addressing these underlying medical concerns may be a prerequisite for fostering effective therapeutic progress within the context of CBT.

The impact of religious or spiritual conflicts cannot be overlooked, particularly when assessing the suitability of CBT. Individuals with strong religious or spiritual beliefs that diverge from the principles of CBT might encounter challenges in embracing cognitive restructuring. In such cases, therapeutic approaches that integrate faith-based counseling or align with the individual's belief system may offer a more congruent therapeutic pathway.

Furthermore, it's important to acknowledge that CBT is generally not intended for acute crisis situations that require immediate intervention and stabilization. Instances where there is an imminent risk of harm to oneself or others necessitate alternate interventions such as crisis management or hospitalization, which take precedence over engaging in CBT.

In conclusion, Cognitive Behavioral Therapy holds a well-deserved position of prominence for its effectiveness in treating a broad spectrum of mental health concerns. However, it is essential to recognize that there are contexts where it may not be the most optimal choice. The decision to pursue CBT or explore alternative therapeutic modalities should be rooted in a comprehensive assessment of individual needs, preferences, and circumstances. Embracing a personalized and holistic approach to mental health treatment remains a cornerstone for achieving optimal therapeutic outcomes.

6) What is the success rate of cognitive behavioral therapy?

The success rate of Cognitive Behavioral Therapy (CBT) varies depending on several factors, including the individual's condition, the therapist's expertise, the client's commitment, and the duration of therapy. However, CBT is generally recognized as one of the most effective forms of psychotherapy and has a substantial body of research supporting its positive outcomes.

For common mental health concerns such as anxiety disorders, depression, and phobias, studies suggest that CBT can lead to significant improvements in most cases. Success rates are often reported to be between 50% to 75%, with some studies indicating even higher rates of success for certain conditions.

It's important to note that "success" in therapy doesn't always mean complete elimination of symptoms. For many, success can be defined as significant symptom reduction, improved coping skills, enhanced emotional regulation, and a better quality of life.

The effectiveness of CBT is enhanced when the therapy is tailored to the individual's needs and when the client actively participates in the therapeutic process.

However, success rates can vary depending on the complexity of the issue and the individual's responsiveness to therapy. Some conditions might require longer-term therapy, additional approaches, or a combination of therapies.

In summary, while exact success rates can't be universally determined, CBT is generally recognized as a highly effective approach to treating a wide range of mental health concerns. Success hinges on factors such as the individual's engagement, therapist-client collaboration, and the adaptability of the therapy to the individual's needs. When well-suited, CBT has the potential to lead to significant and lasting positive changes in an individual's well-being.

7) Does Cognitive Behavioral Therapy help autistics? What are the most effective cognitive behavioral therapy techniques for ADHD?

Cognitive Behavioral Therapy (CBT) has emerged as a promising and impactful approach for individuals with Autism Spectrum Disorder (ASD), offering tailored techniques that have the potential to significantly enhance their quality of life. While the efficacy of CBT in treating ASD can vary based on individual differences, its adaptability and personalized strategies hold immense promise in addressing the diverse range of symptoms and needs associated with the condition.

CBT for ASD is designed to cultivate essential skills that empower individuals to navigate their emotions, enhance social interactions, and improve communication. It's important to emphasize that ASD encompasses a spectrum of experiences, necessitating a customized approach to address the unique challenges and strengths of each individual.

A pivotal focus of CBT for ASD revolves around the development of social skills. Many individuals on the spectrum encounter difficulties in interpreting social cues and engaging in reciprocal conversations. Through techniques like role-playing and real-life scenarios, CBT facilitates the acquisition and practice of these crucial skills, fostering more meaningful and effective social interactions.

Emotion regulation constitutes another significant facet of CBT for ASD. Individuals with ASD may struggle to recognize and express their emotions, often leading to heightened emotional responses. CBT equips them with practical strategies to identify and manage their emotions, promoting emotional well-being and reducing feelings of anxiety or frustration that can frequently accompany ASD.

The cognitive restructuring component of CBT proves particularly valuable for individuals with ASD. By challenging and modifying negative thought patterns, individuals are empowered to address rigid thinking and embrace more flexible problem-solving approaches, ultimately enhancing their adaptability in various situations.

CBT interventions for ASD frequently integrate strategies to manage anxiety, which is a common co-occurring condition. These interventions may include relaxation exercises, gradual exposure to anxiety-inducing situations, and cognitive reframing techniques to alleviate the symptoms of anxiety and provide effective coping mechanisms.

Given the sensory sensitivities often experienced by individuals with ASD, CBT also dedicates attention to sensory challenges. Techniques are employed to help individuals manage sensory overload and sensitivities, resulting in greater comfort and reduced distress within different environments.

The integration of mindfulness and self-awareness practices within CBT for ASD further underscores its holistic approach. These practices cultivate self-awareness, reduce stress, and facilitate emotional regulation by encouraging individuals to become attuned to their emotions, thoughts, and sensory experiences, ultimately promoting a greater sense of well-being.

Family involvement is a fundamental pillar of CBT for ASD, recognizing the crucial role that caregivers play in an individual's journey. Parent training equips caregivers with effective strategies to support their child's development, manage challenging behaviors, and create a structured and supportive home environment. This collaborative effort extends the benefits of CBT beyond therapy sessions, fostering a comprehensive and consistent approach to support.

CBT also addresses executive functioning skills, which are often impaired in individuals with ASD. Techniques aim to enhance skills such as organization, planning, and time management, enabling individuals to navigate daily tasks more effectively and foster greater independence.

Problem-solving skills, honed through CBT, empower individuals with ASD to systematically approach challenges and make informed decisions. These skills contribute to increased self-assuredness and independence, further promoting their overall well-being.

Visual supports, including aids and schedules, play a pivotal role in CBT interventions for ASD. These visual tools enhance communication, aid in understanding routines, and help mitigate anxiety stemming from uncertainty, creating a more structured and manageable environment.

In conclusion, Cognitive Behavioral Therapy (CBT) offers a comprehensive and individualized approach to support individuals with Autism Spectrum Disorder. By tailoring techniques to address specific challenges, CBT empowers individuals to develop social skills, manage emotions, alleviate anxiety, and enhance overall well-being. The personalized and collaborative nature of CBT positions it as a valuable tool in helping individuals with ASD thrive and lead fulfilling lives. Consulting with a qualified therapist specialized in

ASD is essential to create a tailored and effective CBT intervention that meets the unique needs of everyone on the spectrum. Through its versatile and adaptable strategies, CBT holds the potential to significantly enhance the lives of individuals with ASD and contribute to their holistic growth and development.

8) Is Cognitive Behavioral Therapy effective for OCD (Obsessive-compulsive disorder)?

Cognitive Behavioral Therapy (CBT) emerges as a beacon of hope and efficacy in the intricate landscape of Obsessive-Compulsive Disorder (OCD) treatment, offering a transformative path for individuals grappling with the distressing grip of this condition. The pervasive nature of OCD, characterized by distressing obsessions and repetitive compulsions, demands a therapeutic approach that delves deep into the core mechanisms driving these symptoms. CBT, a well-established and evidence-based modality, rises to the occasion, providing a structured and effective framework for individuals to alleviate their distress and regain command over their lives.

Central to CBT for OCD is a two-pronged strategy encompassing cognitive therapy and exposure and response prevention (ERP). This comprehensive approach meticulously addresses the intricate interplay between distressing thoughts and behaviors that fuel the disorder, creating a holistic roadmap for transformative change.

Cognitive therapy, a foundational component of CBT, embarks on a journey through the labyrinth of thought patterns. It involves identifying irrational and anxiety-inducing obsessions that permeate one's mental landscape. Through a collaborative and guided process, individuals unravel these thoughts, meticulously challenging their validity and replacing them with balanced and rational alternatives.

This process of cognitive reframing not only alleviates immediate distress but also equips individuals with the cognitive toolkit necessary to navigate future obsessions with fortified resilience.

The robust efficacy of CBT for OCD finds strong backing in an extensive body of research and clinical trials. These studies consistently highlight the profound impact of CBT in diminishing OCD symptoms and enhancing overall well-being. A significant number of individuals who engage in CBT experience a notable reduction in obsessions, compulsions, and the associated anxiety, resulting in improved functioning across various domains of their lives.

Beyond the immediate treatment period, the benefits of CBT ripple out, casting a lasting influence on an individual's well-being. The skills honed during CBT serve as an enduring armor against potential relapses, equipping individuals with the necessary tools to navigate future challenges and fluctuations in symptom severity. This sustainable approach fosters a sense of empowerment and self-reliance, arming individuals with the capability to navigate the complexities of their condition.

However, it's imperative to acknowledge that the effectiveness of CBT for OCD is most pronounced when facilitated by a qualified mental health professional with specialized expertise in OCD treatment. A skilled therapist collaborates closely with individuals to tailor treatment strategies to their unique symptoms and needs, cultivating a collaborative and supportive therapeutic partnership that maximizes the potential for positive outcomes.

In conclusion, CBT emerges as a compassionate and formidable ally in the battle against Obsessive-Compulsive Disorder. Its multifaceted approach meticulously addresses the intricate web of obsessions and compulsions, guiding individuals toward a life characterized by reduced distress and enhanced functionality. CBT empowers individuals with the tools to confront their fears, challenge distorted thoughts, and rewrite the narrative of OCD. For those navigating the tumultuous terrain of OCD, embarking on a journey guided by CBT holds the potential to usher in profound transformation, offering a path towards renewed well-being and improved quality of life.

9) Can cognitive behavior therapy help with fibromyalgia? And with Insomnia?

Absolutely, Cognitive Behavioral Therapy (CBT) emerges as a promising approach to address the challenges posed by fibromyalgia and insomnia. While these conditions may seem distinct, their shared underlying factors often make them amenable to the principles of CBT. Let's explore how CBT can offer relief and enhanced well-being for individuals grappling with fibromyalgia and insomnia.

Fibromyalgia, characterized by widespread musculoskeletal pain, fatigue, and sleep disturbances, can profoundly impact one's quality of life. CBT steps into this arena by targeting both the physical and psychological dimensions of the condition. It helps individuals understand the intricate interplay between their thoughts, emotions, behaviors, and physical sensations. By identifying and challenging negative thought patterns related to pain and fatigue, CBT empowers individuals to reshape their perceptions and reactions.

CBT for fibromyalgia often incorporates pain management techniques. Individuals learn to implement pacing strategies, which involve balancing activities and rest to manage pain and energy levels effectively. Gradually increasing activity levels while learning to listen to one's body can lead to improved functioning and reduced pain over time. Additionally, relaxation techniques, such as deep breathing and progressive muscle relaxation, help mitigate the muscle tension and stress often accompanying fibromyalgia.

Insomnia, a common companion to fibromyalgia and an independent condition, is another area where CBT shines. Sleep disturbances exacerbate the symptoms of fibromyalgia, creating a vicious cycle of pain and sleeplessness. CBT for insomnia, often referred to as CBT-I, seeks to reestablish healthy sleep patterns by addressing the cognitive and behavioral factors contributing to sleep difficulties.

In the realm of insomnia, CBT delves into sleep hygiene practices, which encompass adopting habits that promote restful sleep. It involves optimizing the sleep environment, establishing a consistent sleep schedule, and minimizing stimulants close to bedtime. Additionally, CBT-I tackles the cognitive aspects of insomnia, such as challenging unrealistic expectations about sleep and addressing the anxiety associated with bedtime.

It's worth noting that CBT for fibromyalgia and insomnia is typically delivered by trained professionals who tailor the approach to the individual's unique circumstances. Collaborative discussions between the therapist and the individual help identify specific triggers, challenges, and goals. By working together, they create a personalized toolkit of strategies that target both the physical and emotional aspects of these conditions.

The effectiveness of CBT in addressing fibromyalgia and insomnia is supported by a growing body of research. Studies consistently highlight the positive impact of CBT on reducing pain, fatigue, sleep disturbances, and overall distress. Moreover, the skills acquired through CBT empower individuals to take an active role in managing their conditions, fostering a sense of control and self-efficacy.

CBT offers a ray of hope for individuals grappling with fibromyalgia and insomnia. Its holistic approach, addressing both the physical and psychological dimensions of these conditions, equips individuals with practical tools to manage pain, fatigue, sleep disturbances, and related emotional distress. CBT's emphasis on self-awareness, resilience, and skill-building empowers individuals to rewrite the narrative of their health and well-being. As always, seeking the guidance of a qualified mental health professional experienced in CBT is crucial for tailoring the approach to individual needs and maximizing the potential for positive outcomes.

10) How AI can be used to make Cognitive Behavioral Therapy (CBT) more effective?

The integration of Artificial Intelligence (AI) into Cognitive Behavioral Therapy (CBT) has ushered in a new era of innovation and effectiveness, revolutionizing the way mental health interventions are delivered. The marriage of AI and CBT holds the potential to enhance accessibility, personalization, and engagement, ultimately making therapy more effective and tailored to individual needs.

One of the remarkable advancements is the emergence of internet-based CBT programs. These platforms offer a range of interactive modules that guide individuals through CBT techniques and exercises at their own pace. AI algorithms analyze user responses, identifying patterns and tailoring the program's content to match everyone's progress and challenges. This adaptability ensures that users receive a personalized therapeutic experience, increasing the likelihood of positive outcomes.

Smartphone applications have also become invaluable tools in the field of AI-assisted CBT. These apps bring therapy to users' fingertips, providing them with on-the-go access to various CBT exercises, mood tracking, and relaxation techniques. AI algorithms embedded within these apps can analyze usage patterns and data, offering insights into users' emotional states and progress. This data-driven approach enables the app to suggest relevant interventions, helping users manage their symptoms in real-time.

Here are some popular smartphone applications that incorporate AI-driven features to assist with Cognitive Behavioral Therapy (CBT) techniques:

o   Woebot: Woebot is an AI-powered chatbot designed to provide emotional support and CBT-based interventions. It offers users personalized conversations, mood tracking, and guided exercises to help manage their mental well-being.

o   Youper: Youper utilizes AI to engage in conversations and track mood patterns. It provides personalized insights and suggests CBT techniques to manage emotions and stress.

o   MoodMission: MoodMission offers a variety of evidence-based CBT strategies to address negative emotions. The app suggests personalized missions aimed at improving mood and reducing distress.

o   Calm: While primarily known for meditation and relaxation, Calm also integrates CBT techniques into its content. It provides mindfulness exercises, breathing techniques, and sleep stories to promote mental well-being.

- o Sanvello: Sanvello offers a range of CBT tools, including mood tracking, guided journeys, and coping strategies for managing stress, anxiety, and depression.
- o Happify: Happify combines positive psychology and CBT techniques to boost emotional well-being. It offers activities and games designed to foster resilience and happiness.
- o SuperBetter: SuperBetter gamifies the process of improving mental health. It encourages users to set goals, complete challenges, and utilize CBT techniques to overcome obstacles and build resilience.
- o CBT-i Coach: Specifically designed for insomnia, CBT-i Coach offers cognitive and behavioral strategies to improve sleep. It helps users develop healthy sleep habits and address sleep-related concerns.
- o Daylio: While not exclusively focused on CBT, Daylio is a mood and habit tracker that can be customized to record daily activities, emotions, and thoughts. This self-awareness tool can complement CBT practices.
- o Wysa: Wysa is an AI-based mental health app that uses CBT techniques and dialectical behavior therapy (DBT) to provide support for stress, anxiety, and mood management.

These applications offer a range of features to support individuals in practicing CBT techniques, managing stress, and improving their mental well-being. It's important to choose an app that aligns with your specific needs and preferences and to complement their use with guidance from a qualified mental health professional if needed.

Virtual reality (VR) has introduced a transformative dimension to CBT. VR-based therapies create immersive environments where individuals can confront and navigate their fears and anxieties in a controlled and safe setting. AI-driven VR systems can adjust the scenarios based on users' reactions and physiological responses, tailoring exposure therapy to the individual's comfort level. This personalized approach enhances the effectiveness of exposure-based interventions, such as treating phobias or post-traumatic stress disorder.

AI's data analysis capabilities extend beyond personalization. By processing large datasets from users' interactions with AI-powered CBT platforms, researchers can uncover insights into the effectiveness of different techniques and interventions. This data-driven approach enables continuous improvement and refinement of therapeutic protocols, ensuring that evidence-based practices are consistently integrated into AI-assisted CBT.

While the benefits of AI-augmented CBT are profound, it's essential to address potential challenges. Privacy and data security remain paramount concerns, as users' sensitive information is collected and analyzed. Robust safeguards and encryption protocols are necessary to ensure that individuals' data is protected.

Additionally, while AI can enhance accessibility to CBT, it should not replace the human element entirely. The therapeutic alliance between a trained mental health professional and the individual is a cornerstone of effective therapy. AI can serve as a complementary tool, offering support between sessions and extending the reach of therapeutic interventions.

AI has brought about a paradigm shift in the field of Cognitive Behavioral Therapy, amplifying its effectiveness and reach. Internet-based programs, smartphone applications, and virtual reality therapies powered by AI algorithms provide personalized and data-driven interventions. These innovations empower individuals to engage in therapy on their terms, enhance the precision of treatment, and offer insights that contribute to the ongoing evolution of CBT. While challenges exist, the synergy between AI and CBT holds the promise of a more accessible, engaging, and effective mental health landscape.

CONCLUSION

As we conclude this book, we have examined the practical applications of Cognitive Behavioral Therapy (CBT) and explored the myriad paths that lead toward heightened awareness, control, and emotional well-being. Throughout its chapters, we have discovered that CBT is not just a therapeutic methodology, but a valuable ally in our journey towards a more balanced and fulfilling life.

Each chapter has unveiled powerful tools and effective techniques that can be adopted by anyone seeking to tackle anxiety, stress, mood disorders, and other mental challenges. From recognizing negative thought patterns to constructing healthy lifestyle habits, from practicing mindfulness to seeking social support, CBT has emerged as a guiding light to enhance our mental health.

However, it is imperative to underscore that the journey toward emotional well-being can vary from person to person. There is no one-size-fits-all solution. Fortunately, CBT offers us an extraordinary arsenal of tools that can be customized and tailored to our specific needs. It is a process that demands commitment, patience, and consistent practice, but the outcomes can be remarkable.

Remember, you are not alone on this journey. Many individuals, professionals, communities, and resources are available to support us along the way. The significance of seeking support, both from friends and family and qualified practitioners, cannot be emphasized enough. Every step forward, no matter how small, brings us closer to a more fulfilling and rewarding life experience.

I hope that this book has served as an illuminating starting point for you, providing fresh perspectives and tangible tools to confront the challenges of everyday life. The path to mental well-being may be winding, but each step we take brings us closer to a stronger, more resilient, and happier version of ourselves.

In conclusion, allow me to share a reflection: the human mind is akin to a garden. It requires care, attention, and constant cultivation to bloom in all its glory. Cognitive Behavioral Therapy is a tool that aids us in tending to this inner garden, confronting the weeds of negative thoughts, and nurturing flowers of hope, resilience, and joy to flourish.

I wish you every success in your journey of growth and healing. May you continue to tend to your mental garden with care, determination, and kindness.

CBT DAILY WORKSHEET

"CBT in Action: Your Daily Workbook: Enhance Your Well-Being Through Practical and User-Friendly CBT Exercises" is a tool designed to empower you with practical exercises and insights that can reshape your thoughts, emotions, and behaviors.

Inside the workbook you will find:

- A **Quick-Start Checklist** to identify current cognitive distortions and specific areas of focus.
- The **Wheel of Life** to assess the balance and satisfaction in various areas of your life.
- A **Setting Goal Card** to help you create a customized path of progress.
- Guided Exercises to practice **Gratitude** and **Meditation** every day.
- The **ABC Model** to gain awareness of thought patterns.
- Worksheets to acknowledge **Positive Moments** in your day, and a **Positive Self-Affirmations list** to rewire your brain into a growth mindset and higher self-esteem.
- A **Behavioral Activation Activities Checklist** to encourage you to engage in meaningful and rewarding activities.
- **Weekly Charts** to rate your commitment on a weekly basis.
- A **Progress Chart** to monitor your personal growth advancement.
- **One Week Template** to help you create the habit of engaging with the exercises regularly.
- A **Monthly Worry Time Worksheet** to learn how to manage anxieties and concerns.
- A **Monthly Anxiety Management Plan**, a 30-day journey to manage anxiety and stress using a variety of effective techniques.

Scan the QR Code to download your FREE BONUS!

SOURCES

- Greenberger, D., & Padesky, C. A. (2015). Mind Over Mood: Change How You Feel by Changing the Way You Think. Guilford Press.

- Neenan, M., & Dryden, W. (2014). Cognitive Behaviour Therapy: 100 Key Points and Techniques. Routledge.

- Linehan, M. M. (2014). DBT Skills Training Manual (Second Edition). Guilford Press.

- Hofmann, S. G., Asnaani, A., Vonk, I. J., Sawyer, A. T., & Fang, A. (2012). The Efficacy of Cognitive Behavioral Therapy: A Review of Meta-analyses. Cognitive Therapy and Research, 36(5), 427-440.

- Hayes, S. C., Strosahl, K. D., & Wilson, K. G. (2012). Acceptance and Commitment Therapy: The Process and Practice of Mindful Change. Guilford Press.

- Beck, J. S. (2011). Cognitive Behavior Therapy: Basics and Beyond. Guilford Press.

- Kliem, S., Kröger, C., Kosfelder, J., & Bailer, J. (2010). Applying the transtheoretical model of change to pre-treatment stage, treatment attendance, and therapeutic alliance during a 6-week cognitive behavioral group therapy for social anxiety disorder. Psychotherapy Research, 20(4), 423-433.

- Wood, A. M., Joseph, S., & Maltby, J. (2008). Gratitude uniquely predicts satisfaction with life: Incremental validity above the domains and facets of the five factor model. Personality and Individual Differences, 45(1), 49-54.

- Ellis, A., & Dryden, W. (2007). The Practice of Rational Emotive Behavior Therapy. Springer Publishing Company.

- Seligman, M. E., Steen, T. A., Park, N., & Peterson, C. (2005). Positive Psychology Progress: Empirical Validation of Interventions. American Psychologist, 60(5), 410-421.

THANK YOU

Dear Readers,

Thank you for choosing my book on Cognitive Behavioral Therapy. Your support means a lot to me.

If you enjoyed the read, I'd greatly appreciate it if you could take a moment to leave a review. Your feedback helps others discover the book and is invaluable to me as an author.

Thank you again, and I hope the book brings you insight and inspiration.

Best regards,

Linda Bextor

ABOUT THE AUTHOR

Meet Linda Bextor, a seasoned explorer of the human mind and emotions. With a profound passion for psychology and a heart that empathizes deeply, she has dedicated her life to helping others navigate their inner landscapes.

At 45, Linda is an accomplished author, weaving her wisdom into books that touch hearts and transform lives. Her first work, "Inner Child Healing" illuminates the path to self-discovery and healing, while her Ultimate Cognitive Behavioral Therapy Guide promises to be a beacon of hope for those seeking positive change.

With an intuitive pen and a nurturing spirit, Linda inspires readers to embrace their true selves and life's journey.

Made in United States
Troutdale, OR
11/04/2023

14301617R00086